BLS WORKING PAPERS

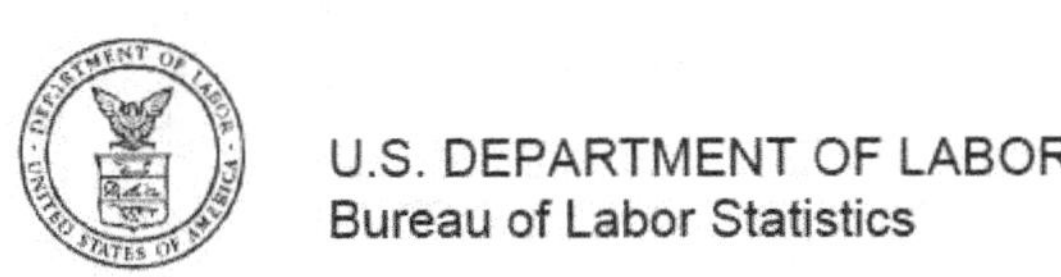

U.S. DEPARTMENT OF LABOR
Bureau of Labor Statistics

OFFICE OF PRODUCTIVITY AND TECHNOLOGY

U.S. Public Infrastructure and Its Contribution to Private Sector Productivity

Aklilu A. Zegeye, U.S. Bureau of Labor Statistics

Working Paper 329
June 2000

U. S. Public Infrastructure and

Its Contribution to Private Sector Productivity

Aklilu A. Zegeye
Bureau of Labor Statistics
e-mail: Zegeye_A@BLS.GOV.

May 15, 2000

The views expressed are those of the author and do not reflect the policies of the U. S. Bureau of Labor Statistics or the views of other staff members. The author is deeply indebted to Larry Rosenblum for his very useful discussions and comments during the preparation of this paper. I would also like to thank Michael Harper and Marilyn Manser for their helpful comments. Any errors are, of course, a nontradable liability of the author.

U. S. Public Infrastructure and
Its Contribution to Private Sector Productivity

By Aklilu A. Zegeye*

Abstract: *The study examines the impact of public infrastructure capital on the productivity of the manufacturing sector for a sample of over 1500 counties and the 50 U. S. states using a translog production function approach. The study also examines productivity convergence across states and across counties. The county level data are chosen as a unit of analysis in order to minimize the impact of the macro-economy on the estimates. The study finds a positive correlation between infrastructure and output at both the state and local levels. The evidence also seems to suggest that the elasticity of public capital on private sector output rises with the level of aggregation. The estimates further show that convergence is occurring faster at the state level than at the county level which has a similar implication of increasing spillover with the level of aggregation. However, the study finds that even though public infrastructure does have an impact on output and productivity at both the state and county levels, its influence on productivity is small.*

(JEL CODE: H54 &R00)

* The Bureau of Labor Statistics, Division of Productivity Research, 2 Massachusetts Avenue NE, Washington, DC 20212. The author is deeply indebted to Larry Rosenblum for his very useful discussions and comments during the preparation of this paper. I would also like to thank Michael Harper and Marilyn Manser for their helpful comments. Any errors are, of course, a nontradable liability of the author.

U. S. Public Infrastructure and Its

Contribution to Private Sector Productivity

The study examines the impact of public infrastructure capital on the productivity of the manufacturing sector for a sample of over 1500 counties and the 50 U. S. states using a translog production function approach. The study also examines productivity convergence across states and across counties. The county level data are chosen as a unit of analysis in order to minimize the impact of the macro-economy on the estimates. The study finds a positive correlation between infrastructure and output at both the state and local levels. The evidence also seems to suggest that the elasticity of public capital on private sector output rises with the level of aggregation. The estimates further show that convergence is occurring faster at the state level than at the county level which has a similar implication of increasing spillover with the level of aggregation. However, the study finds that even though public infrastructure does have an impact on output and productivity at both the state and county levels, its influence on productivity is small.

(JEL CODE: H54 &R00)

I. INTRODUCTION

A number of studies have examined the relationship between public sector infrastructure capital and its contribution to private sector productivity.[1] There is little doubt that public sector infrastructure affects private sector production by increasing aggregate demand and by augmenting productivity and output.[2]

One important source of disagreement in the literature arises from choices in the level of aggregation. By and large, the reported elasticities of infrastructure on output at different levels of aggregation are mixed. The findings frequently imply under-investment in infrastructure, but the evidence is far from firm and thus hardly conclusive. At the national and state levels, the macro economic effects of any spending including infrastructure may dominate the positive

[1] Using national, regional, metropolitan, state and industry level data, studies by Eberts (1986), Aschauer (1989), Munnell (1990), Garcia Mila and McGuire(1992), Morrison and Schwartz (1992), and Nadiri and Mamuneas (1994) have shown a significant contribution of public capital to private sector productivity. On the other hand, using regional and state data, Hulten and Schwab (1993), Evans and Karras (1994), Holtz-Eakin (1994) find no evidence that public capital growth leads to greater productivity growth. Hulten and Schwab (1984, 1993), Eisner (1991), and Munnell (1990) did regional studies by breaking down states into four regions (northeast, north central, south, and west) while Meira (1975) divided the 48 states into 9 US census regions. Eberts (1986), Deno and Eberts (1989) using a translog production function, and Deno (1988) using a translog profit function estimated the effects of some of the components of public sector capital stock on regional manufacturing output for 38 metropolitan areas, while Nadiri and Mamuneas (1991) estimated a cost function at an industry level using twelve two digit US manufacturing industries. Deno and Eberts (1989) estimated for 28 SMSAs for the first half of the 1980s using 2SLS rather than OLS to avoid simultaneity bias that can arise between private income and public investment. See Gramlich's (1994) survey article for a range of estimates and some of the issues.

[2] See Tatom (1991) and Holtz-Eakin (1993b) who have examined a number of issues such as fixed effects, specification of error structure, endogeneity bias, restrictions on the coefficients to satisfy constant returns to scale, and the effects of aggregation.

externalities of spending on production. Specifically, public spending may increase aggregate demand and provide stimulus to the economy. However, this result may not be unique to infrastructure. In such cases, the resultant correlation between public spending and private sector output may not be the result of the public good nature of public capital. Second, public sector spending may be a normal good. That is, as income rises the demand for public infrastructure increases so that the correlation between infrastructure and output may reflect the marginal propensity to consume public goods rather than any productivity enhancing effects of infrastructure.

This paper seeks to address these concerns by examining manufacturing production at the county level. While state output has its own components that are not tied to the aggregate economy, large states are clearly affected by national trends. In general, counties are the smallest geographical areas for which significant amounts of data are available. Since output is less correlated across counties than across states and regions, analysis of infrastructure at the more disaggregated levels are more likely to measure the impact of infrastructure on output rather than the marginal propensity to spend tax revenues on infrastructure.[3]

We will estimate fixed effect models to eliminate unobservable productivity differences such as natural resource endowments and air and water quality as well as further test their differences using more broadly defined regional categories (north, south, east and west) as dummy variables. The study will also address the issue of productivity performance and productivity convergence across U. S. counties.

Furthermore, to examine the possible existence of differences of productivity of manufacturing due to the degree of urbanization, the study uses Beale's codes for U. S. counties

[3] At the county level, national influences are considerably muted and the correlation between county level growth and national growth are much weaker.

(which divide counties into 10 demographic regions depending on the degree of urbanization and nearness to a metro area) as dummy variables. [4]

Because there are no comprehensive measures of private and public capital stock, to my knowledge, available at the county level, this study will construct a measure of public and private capital stocks based on the perpetual inventory technique. This approach improves on the use of current capital outlays or adding up a short series of past capital expenditures. It further weakens any correlation between infrastructure spending and aggregate stimulus.

In section 2, we begin by sketching the model which provides the basis for analysis, discussing appropriate estimation techniques. The sources and description of data are discussed in section 3, while section 4 presents the empirical results of these estimates and their effects on productivity. In section 5, we discuss productivity performance and productivity convergence across U. S. counties, while the final section is a summary.

II. METHOD OF ANALYSIS

Aggregate production relates the gross state or county manufacturing output (Q) to four inputs: private capital (K), workers (L), intermediate materials (M), public sector capital (G) and the level of technology, and thus Q = F(L, M, K, G, t). A Translog production function in its unrestricted form is:[5]

$$\ln Q = \beta_0 + \beta_L \ln L + \beta_K \ln K + \beta_M \ln M + \beta_G \ln G + \frac{1}{2}\beta_{LL} \ln L^2 + \frac{1}{2}\beta_{KK} \ln K^2$$
$$+ \frac{1}{2}\beta_{MM} \ln M^2 + \frac{1}{2}\beta_{GG} \ln G^2 + \beta_{LK} \ln K \ln L + \beta_{LM} \ln M \ln L + \beta_{KM} \ln M \ln K + \quad (1)$$
$$\beta_{GL} \ln G \ln L + \beta_{GM} \ln M \ln G + \beta_{KG} \ln K \ln G$$

---

[4] See Butler (1990) for details of Beale's code grouping. The coefficients of these variables will measure systematic effects of amenities associated with congestion (versus open space). According to McGuckin and Peck (1992), the Beale codes grouping (also known as rural-urban continuum codes) which is published by the Department of Agriculture is a much finer residential grouping than the traditional census metropolitan and non-metropolitan classification.

[5] The production function is twice differentiable and is modified to include public sector infrastructure as an "externality" factor. The production function is decreasing and convex in the three input quantities, but increasing and concave in G. We assume changes in G result in costs of adjustments. See Guilkey et al (1983) for the demonstarted superiority of the translog functional form over the alternate functional forms. Kaizuka (1965) is the first to introduce public capital as one of the inputs, besides labor and capital, in a private production function.

A well behaved production (a factor demand) function must be homogeneous of degree one (zero) in quantities. Symmetry $(\beta_{ij} = \beta_{ji})$ and Hick's neutrality are imposed *a priori* in the specification of (1). Depending on the specific model, constant returns to scale in either the private or all inputs including public inputs is imposed. The corresponding income shares of labor and capital are defined, respectively, as:

$$S_L = \left(\frac{P_L L}{P_Q Q}\right) = \frac{L}{Q}\left(\frac{\partial Q}{\partial L}\right) = \left(\frac{\partial \ln Q}{\partial \ln L}\right) = \beta_L + \beta_{LL} \ln L + \beta_{LK} \ln K + \beta_{ML} \ln M + \beta_{GL} \ln G$$

$$S_K = \left(\frac{P_K K}{P_Q Q}\right) = \frac{K}{Q}\left(\frac{\partial Q}{\partial K}\right) = \left(\frac{\partial \ln Q}{\partial \ln K}\right) = \beta_K + \beta_{KK} \ln K + \beta_{LK} \ln L + \beta_{MK} \ln M + \beta_{KG} \ln G \qquad (2)$$

To account for state- and county-specific fixed effects, variables are entered in the translog production function as deviations from their state- or county-specific means. For example, the observation vectors for each county involve differences for each county's value from the mean which is generated using all the counties under study in that state.[6]

The production function and input shares depend not only on input quantities, output and technological change, but also on public infrastructure capital. The spill-over effects of public sector capital on cost and input shares are captured by the magnitudes and signs of the parameters $(\beta_G, \beta_{GG}, \beta_{GL}, \beta_{KG}, \beta_{MG})$. Thus the infrastructure impact is determined by the derivative of the production function with respect to public capital. We calculate the elasticity or the shadow share for public infrastructure as:

$$S_G = \left(\frac{Z_G G}{P_Q Q}\right) = \frac{G}{Q}\left(\frac{\partial Q}{\partial G}\right) = \left(\frac{\partial \ln Q}{\partial \ln G}\right) = \beta_G + \beta_{GG} \ln G + \beta_{GK} \ln K + \beta_{MG} \ln M + \beta_{GL} \ln L \qquad (3a)$$

[6] See Munnell (1990) and Holtz-Eakin (1992) for details. This study assumes fixed effects are the same for all counties within a state. Another less restrictive method which this study pursues later is to take the first difference between two time periods.

From which the shadow price for public capital is calculated as:

$$Z_G = \left(\frac{P_Q Q}{G}\right)\left(\beta_G + \beta_{GG}\ln G + \beta_{GK}\ln K + \beta_{MG}\ln M + \beta_{GL}\ln L\right) \tag{3b}$$

The parameters in (3b) on public capital should be interpreted as a measure of the marginal product of infrastructure on manufacturing. Because the model is estimated using the manufacturing sector only, the total return (or social return) to aggregate production may well be larger since it includes both the returns to manufacturing and nonmanufacturing establishments as well as individuals.[7]

The production model has three equations--the output equation and the labor and private capital share equations (the share of intermediate input is generated as a residual). These equations share some of the same parameters and are estimated jointly with the appropriate cross restrictions using either the Zellner's Iterative Seemingly Unrelated Regressions (ITSUR) technique, iterated three stage least square method or iterated ordinary least squares method with demographic and regional dummies. They are also estimated in a first difference and pooled cross-section regression format.

The study also tests the appropriateness of the degree to which the estimated production function satisfies the assumption of constant returns to scale (CRTS) in the private inputs (i.e., $S_M + S_K + S_L = 1$), or constant returns to scale in all the inputs including public infrastructure (i.e., $S_M + S_K + S_L + S_G = 1$).

It is now common practice to estimate production functions using the dual rather than the primal form.[8] We have not chosen to do so because the dual relies heavily on the quality of the price data. County level price deflators for output or intermediate inputs do not exist in our data and so we have had to rely on state-level price data and county-level composition to estimate county level prices. As a result,

[7] The difference between the social benefits or the shadow price (Z_G) and social user cost of public capital (P_G) indicates public capital investment opportunities. When marginal products exceed the price, additional investment is warranted. Firms do not pay directly for public capital and thus the price (P_G) is taken to be zero to the firm. For society at large, however, the price (P_G) is non-zero.

[8] See Griliches (1967), Nadiri (1970), Friedlander (1990) and Morrison and schwartz(1992) for a discussion of the dual form and its advantages.

there is little variation in input prices at the county level. However, expenditure data are directly observable for counties and so we believe that estimation of the primal rather than the dual is preferable.

In addition, state level price data limit information available to the translog functional form at the county level. For example, since the state deflators for materials are being used as county deflators, the translog interaction term estimates between materials and the other inputs for the counties could not have revealed any additional information compared with the state estimates. Nevertheless, some county level price and quantity data are available and so the translog form can maximize the use of information compared to more restrictive forms such as Cobb-Douglas and CES.

III. DATA CONSTRUCTION AND DESCRIPTION

We assemble data on the prices and quantities of outputs and inputs of workers, private capital and intermediate materials for the states and 1514 counties from the quincennial Census of Manufactures (CM) for aggregate manufacturing and corresponding public infrastructure capital from the Census of Government (CG) publications for 1982, 1987 and 1992.[9] This data is part of a research effort aimed at creating a complete set of state and county accounts for inputs and outputs as well as the different types of public infrastructure at the two digit and aggregate manufacturing levels. The purpose of these accounts is to allocate U. S. manufacturing growth and productivity to its different sources at the state and local levels.

Every five years, both CG and CM programs under the Department of Commerce provide comprehensive statistics on all units of government, their forms and activities, and all multi-unit and single-unit manufacturing establishments production and input usage, using a nationally consistent set of definitions and classification. Data from complete censuses are used because annual surveys (for example, Annual Survey of Manufactures (ASM)) are designed to measure activity by industry at the national level while census data can be used for county level analysis as well.

[9] BEA, Census of Government, Census of Manufactures have not only been the source of our data, but Mr. Henry Wulf (Census of Government) and Mr. Tim Dobbs (Bureau of Economic Analysis (BEA)) have been extremely helpful in clarifying definitional and procedural issues concerning data collection of respective data sets.

The sample of states and 1514 counties is constrained by the availability of consistent private capital stock estimates for the three census years. Although it would have been desirable to use a four-, a three-, or even a two-digit manufacturing SIC as our frame of analysis, confidentiality requirements by industry at the county level are quite severe and the remaining sample would not have been representative. Moreover, there is no theoretical guidance for apportioning infrastructure assets into the different sectors of the economy (e.g. agriculture, manufacturing, etc.) let alone ferreting out the different responses of each industry within manufacturing to expanded provision of infrastructure. Therefore, the analysis is limited to total manufacturing in each state and county under study. State level aggregates were then adjusted to reflect BEA or BLS estimates of the national totals. However, such data controls were not available for the county level data since not all counties in each state were included in our sample.

IIIA. OUTPUT AND INTERMEDIATE INPUTS

We begin with state and county series for value of shipments in current dollars obtained from CM as a measure of gross product. According to Norsworthy and Malmquist (1982), the gross output specification puts less restrictions on the production function than does value-added. As a production concept, value-added is appropriate only if there is perfect competition. The implicit assumption for using a value-added specification is that capital and labor are separable from their intermediate inputs and further precludes it from the growth accounting approach. According to Basu and Fernald (1997), value-added does not, in general, capture the "net" contribution of primary input and technology to output. Therefore, we use the gross state and county product; consistent with gross output, capital and labor, and intermediate inputs are used.

The price deflator for manufacturing output for each state is calculated as a weighted average of BLS national 2-digit output prices using state specific industry output share weights for each year.[10] Because county level output deflators are not available from any sources, these

[10] Because a complete set of county output data are unavailable , county level weights cannot be constructed and used.

state output deflators are also used to deflate the county gross outputs. If the law of one price within the states does not hold, county prices are changing relative to the respective state deflators, or the composition of output within industries varies across counties, then state manufacturing deflators will misstate real county output. However, these estimates improve upon the national output deflators used in past studies.

The data for intermediate inputs include all purchased materials and fuels. The material costs from Census data are much less than BEA's intermediate input. Census attributes more of total output to value-added while BEA allocates more to intermediates, which include purchased business services. Accordingly, the material values from the Census have been adjusted to include the actual dollar value of purchased business services from the BLS KLEMS MFP database.[11] The BLS national total has been apportioned to each state and county in proportion to its share of materials in the Census data. Consequently, the gross state product has been increased to account for these changes.

The deflators for materials at the state level were calculated using double deflation of gross output and value-added. That is, real gross output minus real value-added equals the real value of materials. From this, the price of materials is the ratio of nominal to real materials. The deflator used for value-added in each state is the ratio of nominal to real GSP from BEA's Gross State Product (GSP). Because county level materials deflators are not available from any sources, these state deflators are also used to deflate the county intermediate inputs.

IIIB. LABOR

In general, labor input for each state and county is measured as a Tornqvist index of total hours worked for production and non-production workers, while the hourly compensation for production and non-production workers are used to form cost share weights. The CM contains the hours paid and employment of production workers for establishments, but only employment of

[11] See Gullickson (1992) for details.

non-production workers. Because hours paid are a more accurate measure of labor input than employment, we develop estimates of hours worked for non-production workers. To convert the employment of non-production workers to an estimate of hours worked, we multiply the number of non-production workers by the average annual hours of production workers.

Furthermore, the CM reports gross earnings of all employees and all production workers in each manufacturing establishment in each calendar year. Gross earnings of non-production workers is the difference between these two. The price index for labor input is, therefore, the total payroll divided by the Tornqvist index of total hours (L).

IIIC. CAPITAL

The appropriate measure of capital is capital stock rather than investment. Because services flow from the entire stock of capital, rather than just new investment, stocks represent a more complete picture of capital used as inputs to production. This is especially true in the case of public capital where the standards for investment are not the same as in the private sector.[12]

Because the construction of the public sector capital series proceeded much like the private capital series, we will discuss the general features of both before we discuss the specifics of each. The database for state and county investment for U. S. total manufacturing industries comes from the Census of Manufactures (CM) (Report by Geographic Regions); the database for the public capital outlay for the states and counties was obtained from the Census of Government publications (CG) report. Data are available for 1982, 1987 and 1992. Capital stocks are commonly measured using "vintage aggregation" or a "perpetual inventory method" which uses gross investment in constant dollars, an initial benchmark for the capital stock and a depreciation rate or service life estimate. Therefore, estimating private and public capital stocks for the non-census years require estimating capital outlays for each state and county.

[12] See Michael Boskin, et al (1987) for details.

Investment was interpolated assuming that the annual values follow a geometric growth rate between census years 1982, 1987 and 1992. The state investment values for both private and public capital for each year have been controlled by the national totals. If investment in a census year for the public sector was zero, the interpolation is done by assuming that the annual values follow a linear path.

Moreover, since we have actual private sector data for the states from 1988 to 1991 (from 1992 Census of Manufactures Area and Industry series), these actual state values are used as a control to interpolate county private investment values for those years. The basic idea is to scale the observed county-level growth rates to be consistent with observed state-level growth. This formula works well provided that the state changes in growth rates were not too large. Two additional assumptions were imposed on the interpolation of the 1988 to 1991 period. A county could not average more than three times its respective state's growth rate over the 1987-92 period and a county level growth estimate could not exceed 99% or be less than –50%.

Capital stocks measures that are based on the perpetual inventory method need a continuous gross investment series in constant dollars, a constant (geometric) depreciation rate and a benchmark for the capital stock. We will first discuss these derivations for the private capital stock series.

IIIC.1. Private Capital

The physical capital stock is defined as the sum of the stocks of structures or equipment. The nominal investment data for the manufacturing sector (undifferentiated by asset type) were converted to real 1992 dollars, by developing state level investment deflators. The ratio of the state investment deflator to the national deflator was assumed to be proportional to the ratio of state to national value-added deflators.

The private capital stock at the end of each period, K_t, is estimated as a weighted sum of investments of age s at time t $\{I_{t-s}\}$:

$$K_t = \sum_{s=0}^{\infty} \Phi(s) I_{t-s} \qquad (4)$$

where s is service life of the asset and Φ(s) is the relative efficiency index of an s year old asset.[13] We assume that depreciation occurs at a constant (geometric) rate (δ) in which case the relative efficiency index could be expressed as:[14]

$$\Phi(s) = (1-\delta)^s \qquad (5)$$

Therefore, by substitution of equation (5) into equation (4), the formula to estimate capital stock is:

$$K_t = \sum_{s=0}^{\infty} (1-\delta)^s I_{t-s}$$

(6)

The depreciation rates for equipment and structures for the state and county manufacturing sector are imputed from national level data by inverting the perpetual inventory method to solve for the national depreciation rate:

$$\delta = 1 - [K_t - I_t]/K_{t-1} = -\{ [K_t - K_{t-1} - I_t] / K_{t-1} \}. \qquad (7)$$

IIIC.2. Computation of the benchmark private capital stock in 1982

To determine an initial capital stock, we assume a county's share of the total capital stock in 1982 is proportional to its share of total capital payments (value of shipments minus payroll and cost of materials) in 1982.[15] The productive capital stock of 1982 benchmark was apportioned into equipment and structures at the state and county levels in the same proportion as stocks at the national level.

Aggregate capital input for the private sector (K) is computed as a Tornqvist index of equipment and structures stocks, with the share weights employing national level estimates of rental prices for total manufacturing taken from the Capital Measurement Program of the Office of Technology and Productivity in the Bureau of Labor Statistics.[16] It uses a Hall-Jorgenson

---

[13] See Trends in Multifactor Productivity, 1948-1981," BLS Bulletin 2178 for details.

[14] BLS uses a more complex hyperbolic age-efficiency function, but given all the assumptions required here, geometric decay is sufficient.

[15] This is equivalent to the assumption of the rental price being the same across counties in 1982.

[16] See Multifactor Productivity Trends, 1997 (March 1999).

rental price measured as the sum of an implicit rate of return to capital, a rate of depreciation, and capital gains, all adjusted for taxes. Capital income for equipment is then the product of national rental price and state or county capital stock. The income shares of equipment and structures for each year are the ratio of each asset type income to all capital income:

$$S^{STR,YR,j} = \frac{r^{STR,YR,j} K^{STR,YR,j}}{r^{STR,YR,j} K^{STR,YR,j} + r^{Eq,YR,j} K^{Eq,YR,j}}$$

$$and \quad S^{Eq,YR,j} = \frac{r^{Eq,YR,j} K^{Eq,YR,j}}{r^{STR,YR,j} K^{STR,YR,j} + r^{Eq,YR,j} K^{Eq,YR,j}} \qquad (8)$$

where j stands for state or county and

$r^{STR,YR,j}$ and $r^{Eq,YR,j}$ represent the national rental prices of structures and equipment, respectively, for aggregate manufacturing and $K^{STR,YR,j}$ and $K^{Eq,YR,j}$ are real capital stocks of structures and equipment for each state or county, respectively. Tornqvist indexes of state and county total capital stocks are created using these imputed capital income asset shares.

The aggregate price of capital services P_K for the manufacturing sector is computed as capital payments (=gross output-materials-payroll) divided by the Tornqvist quantity index, K. Our estimate of the net private capital stock in 1992 dollars and their rental prices for the 50 states for the census years 1982, 1987, and 1992 are displayed in Table 1.

Table 1
Estimates of Private Capital Stocks and Capital service Prices by State
(unit: Millions of 1992 Dollars, price index, 1992=1)

State Name	Private K 1982	Rental P_K 1982	Private K 1987	Rental P_K 1987	Private K 1992	Rental P_K 1992
ALABAMA	6747.5	0.8035	7639.8	1.1187	9671.3	1.0
ALASKA	513.3	0.6615	546.4	0.5195	592.1	1.0
ARIZONA	5644.9	0.4481	6767.1	0.7626	7803.4	1.0
ARKANSAS	5225.9	0.7317	5568.6	0.8577	6069.1	1.0
CALIFORNIA	67334.5	0.6211	70663.3	0.8171	72977.6	1.0
COLORADO	5700.4	0.5458	6493.7	0.8548	7122.1	1.0
CONNECTICUT	9203.4	0.6582	9569.9	0.9021	10034.4	1.0
DELAWARE	832.2	0.9606	879.7	1.1997	969.2	1.0
FLORIDA	13147.5	0.6401	14362.3	0.8566	14813.2	1.0
GEORGIA	14148.4	0.5939	16349.6	0.9567	18705.2	1.0
HAWAII	1422.9	0.8034	1580.8	0.9978	2005.0	1.0
IDAHO	1224.0	0.8070	1292.9	1.0441	1712.0	1.0
ILLINOIS	27855.6	0.7207	29085.8	0.9395	30934.3	1.0
INDIANA	16382.6	0.6501	18759.5	0.9128	21849.6	1.0
IOWA	10252.3	0.5716	9677.5	0.6738	10045.7	1.0
KANSAS	5653.5	0.6495	6236.7	0.8660	6460.7	1.0
KENTUCKY	10400.5	0.5503	12107.7	0.7150	13379.8	1.0
LOUISIANA	4418.6	0.8627	6562.6	1.1404	8845.8	1.0
MAINE	1512.2	1.2007	1786.3	1.2843	2033.5	1.0
MARYLAND	6336.2	0.6526	6600.9	0.9242	7124.7	1.0
MASSACHUSETTS	16291.2	0.7170	16160.0	1.0167	15852.6	1.0
MICHIGAN	15248.6	0.7910	19370.2	0.8996	23151.5	1.0
MINNESOTA	8294.2	0.7475	9190.7	1.0448	10263.2	1.0
MISSISSIPPI	5327.5	0.7456	5607.9	0.8325	6239.9	1.0
MISSOURI	14196.1	0.4987	15220.9	0.7166	15939.6	1.0
MONTANA	957.3	0.6895	1048.8	1.2365	1164.8	1.0
NEBRASKA	3260.9	0.5887	3176.6	0.7454	3285.8	1.0
NEVADA	612.3	0.6888	671.6	0.8514	725.8	1.0
NEW HAMPSHIRE	3097.2	0.6149	3009.3	1.5787	2981.6	1.0
NEW JERSEY	18560.8	0.6805	18845.1	0.9574	19448.9	1.0
NEW MEXICO	1546.5	0.4140	1765.7	0.3758	2218.6	1.0
NEW YORK	43035.4	0.6735	41961.7	0.8692	41218.2	1.0
NORTH CAROLINA	29237.6	0.4643	32695.2	0.7187	35004.9	1.0
NORTH DAKOTA	1033.7	0.7951	1096.1	1.2554	1170.9	1.0
OHIO	31725.5	0.6297	34345.8	0.8285	37848.5	1.0
OKLAHOMA	5880.7	0.4651	6401.3	0.6520	7003.1	1.0
OREGON	4398.2	0.7565	4721.3	1.0241	5571.3	1.0
PENNSYLVANIA	26814.0	0.6680	27691.7	0.8377	29541.7	1.0
RHODE ISLAND	2403.7	0.7035	2308.3	0.7987	2186.8	1.0
SOUTH CAROLINA	8061.3	0.6672	9371.9	0.9064	11157.6	1.0
SOUTH DAKOTA	979.4	0.5392	934.9	0.6633	955.0	1.0
TENNESSEE	13273.8	0.6565	14372.3	0.8898	16789.5	1.0
TEXAS	25282.4	0.8661	28835.9	0.9090	34226.6	1.0
UTAH	2497.6	0.6014	2773.2	0.7162	3160.9	1.0
VERMONT	1255.3	0.8216	1484.5	0.7447	1774.6	1.0
VIRGINIA	17925.5	0.4850	19117.5	0.6893	19980.0	1.0
WASHINGTON	3944.5	0.6701	5618.2	0.8920	8861.5	1.0
WEST VIRGINIA	2346.4	0.6709	2696.1	0.9806	3248.0	1.0
WISCONSIN	16740.4	0.6016	16978.3	0.7953	18355.2	1.0
WYOMING	1795.4	0.6708	1892.4	0.3036	1969.0	1.0
TOTAL	**539,980.3**		**581,894.5**		**634,444.2**	

IIIC.3. Public Capital

Public capital is defined as all capital outlays of state and local governments. Capital outlays are available for the years 1982, 1987 and 1992. Construction of the public sector capital series from the Census of Government follows the private sector capital. Total capital outlays by asset types and capital outlays for selected governmental functions of states are reconciled to national level infrastructure capital outlays. These investments by asset types and for certain governmental functions by state and counties were deflated using national level price defaltors derived from BEA data. Therefore, at each level of government, stock measures can be developed for both aggregate public capital accumulation and capital devoted to specific functions (or "core" public infrastructure):-highways, utilities, sanitation, conservation and development, sewerage systems and education.

State and local public stocks of physical assets consists of equipment, land and structures. The stock of capital for each public sector asset by function is computed using the perpetual inventory method. For government nonresidential structures and producers durable equipment, the service lives come from BEA's Fixed Reproducible Tangible Wealth, while the depreciation rates come from BLS' Capital Measurement Program. Land is assumed infinitely lived.

The BEA service lives used for the various asset types of state and local government capital are: equipment 15 years; educational, hospital and "other" buildings, 50 years; conservation and development, highways and streets, sewer and water structures, 60 years; and "other" structures, 50 years. These estimated service lives for the various types of state and local government capital are used to infer depreciation rates obtained from BLS.

While there are state and local government asset service lives for structures by function from BEA, there are no published state and local government service lives for equipment by function except by asset types. The depreciation patterns of public equipment likely resemble those of private assets. Therefore, the service lives for the state and local publicly owned equipment is synthesized by averaging the different service lives of similar assets that are privately owned. Also infrastructure stocks are over 90 percent structures and so information on the types of equipment is not vital.[17]

Table 2 shows the depreciation rates (δ) that are assigned to public sector durable equipment and nonresidential structures by function:

---

[17] For example, Aschauer (1989) bifurcated total nonmilitary capital stocks into structures and equipment so that they have separate effects on productivity; and found that structures (93% of the stock) is of primary importance to productivity and could be a good proxy for total nonmilitary public capital stocks.

Table 2
Depreciation Rates of Public Capital by Function and Asset Types

	Equipment	**Structures**
Education	0.1918	0.0348
Hospitals	0.1508	0.0348
Highways and Streets	0.1239	0.0285
Conservation & Development	0.1239	0.0285
Sewer Systems	0.1508	0.0285
Water System	0.1168	0.0285
Other	0.1624	0.0285

IIIC.4. Computation of the benchmark public capital stock in 1982

The initial 1982 public infrastructure capital stock by function is generated by assuming that the ratio of each states' public capital stock ($G_{s,j,82}$) to the national public capital stock ($G_{N,j,82}$) by function is proportional to the ratio of each state's public expenditure ($E_{s,j,82}$)to the national public expenditure ($E_{N,j,82}$) by function. That is, $G_{s,j,82}=\Phi_{s,j,82}* G_{N,82}$.[18]

The 1982 benchmark capital stock is apportioned between equipment and structures for each function by using the aggregate shares for each function across all states. These estimates are then reconciled to national totals. Incidentally, 97 percent of infrastructure stocks are structures in 1982 which suggests that we would not lose much information in our estimates even if we work only with structures.

The next stage in the construction of public capital measurement is the estimation of rental prices or user cost. The before-tax rental price is the sum of a rate of return (r_G) in the form of opportunity costs plus depreciation costs(δ_G) less capital gains or losses arising from changing asset prices:

$$\frac{C_t}{P_t}=r_t+\delta_t-\frac{\Delta P_t}{P_t} \tag{9}$$

[18] This is equivalent to assuming that capital output ratio for each state function is identical across states. N stands for all states or national value, s represents state or county and j stands for governmental function.

Since public capital income is not observable, rental prices cannot be determined from observed data. Instead, we assume county governments optimize on behalf of their citizens. We also assume that governments do not intend to resell assets. Accordingly, capital gains, $\Delta P_t/P_t$, are irrelevant to the rental price calculations. Furthermore, counties do not pay taxes and so tax effects can be ignored. Finally, since we cannot determine an ex-post internal rate of return, we use a 20-year tax-exempt state and local bonds rate of interest (or high grade municipal bond) as the opportunity cost for county governments. Given the simplified rental price formula and that most assets are long-lived structures, rental price will not vary much across most assets. Regardless, Tornqvist indexes of county assets are created using these simplified rental prices to impute capital income asset shares. Table 3 shows the values used for rate of return (r_G), and depreciation rate (δ_G) variables that compute the rental prices of public capital.

Table 3

State and Local Bond Rates (r_G) and Depreciation Rates (δ_G)

Used in the Calculation of the Rental Prices

	1982		**1987**		**1992**	
	Bond Rates	**Depreciation Rates**	**Bond Rates**	**Depreciation Rates**	**Bond Rates**	**Depreciation Rates**
Construction	0.1157	0.1544	0.0773	0.1610	0.0641	0.1634
Equipment	0.1157	0.0204	0.0773	0.0214	0.0641	0.0236
Education	0.1157	0.0144	0.0773	0.0144	0.0641	0.0149
Conservation and Development	0.1157	0.0154	0.0773	0.0154	0.0641	0.0163
Highways &Streets	0.1157	0.0186	0.0773	0.0186	0.0641	0.0163
Utlility, Sewerage and Sanitation	0.1157	0.0155	0.0773	0.0155	0.0641	0.0155

It is important to note some of the differences in private and public sector capital inputs. Unlike private inputs, public capital is a collective input which is shared not only by manufacturing firms but also by other industries and residents of the region as well. The amount of public capital that the manufacturing sector employs (or any sector for that matter) is less than the total amount of public capital of the region. Since this cannot be observed, values of the entire public capital will be used and the average effect for all public capital is measured.

After constructing private and public capital for counties and states for the three census years, these data, together with other inputs, are used to estimate a production function along with its share equations (equations 1 and 2). The sample employed more than 1500 counties. Since some counties are not included in our sample (because not all counties have manufacturing plants), we aggregated these 1514 counties into approximate state measures--'pseudo-states' and compared these aggregates to actual data for the 50 states. The results of the actual state and pseudo-state data were very similar, and accordingly, we report the actual state data regression results.

IV. Estimation Results

The estimation of the effect of public capital on the gross output at the state and county levels is based on the construction of public and private capital stock series. These state-by-state and county-by-county capital series provide data for each of the 50 states in the U. S. and a little over 1500 counties for the census years 1982, 1987 and 1992.[19] There are 3040 counties in the U. S.; half were omitted because either they had no manufacturing plants during the 1982-1992 period or confidentiality prohibited the Census from reporting the data. However, as a group, the counties under study accounted for at least 80% of total state gross output and at least 85% to 90% of the total state private capital in manufacturing in those three census years (see Table 4 below), but only for half of the total states' public infrastructure capital stock. Therefore, the distribution of private capital in manufacturing is more concentrated than the distribution of public infrastructure capital. This might be an indication that public resources are allocated by some other means rather than profit maximization, as is mostly done in private sector inputs.

Comparing the state and county public capital by type of asset, Table 4 also reveals that highways, education and conservation are principally financed at the state level, whereas utilities, sewerage and sanitation are funded mostly by local governments. According to Michael Boskin, et al (1987), highways and education building account for 57 percent of total state and local government nonresidential capital. In this study, after bifurcating the state and local capital, highways and education buildings account for

[19] See Appendix Tables 1 and 2 for the 50 states and the largest 100 counties, stacked according to their private capital stocks, for the values of their private and public capital for the three census years. Annex Table 3 presents private and public capital stocks for the same census years for over 1500 counties by state considered for the study.

over 50 percent of state capital, whereas they account for only a little over 30 percent of county capital for the three census years.[20]

Table 4

Total State and County Private Capital and Public Capital Stocks

As well as Public Capital Stocks by Type of Asset

(millions of 1992 dollars)

	STATE			COUNTY		
	1982	**1987**	**1992**	**1982**	**1987**	**1992**
Private capital	535344.0	577572.0	630043.6	487870.0	508769.7	535415.5
Public capital	222778.6	247811.3	282721.5	105644.9	115691.0	131824.7
Education	41343.3	44311.0	52046.6	15942.1	17679.8	22702.0
Highways and Streets	75282.8	80313.2	88498.1	18140.3	19126.8	20789.2
Utilities	15891.5	21253.1	27117.2	11578.1	15842.0	20561.1
Sewerage	16881.5	18952.1	21354.8	14742.6	16475.0	18474.9
Sanitation	1695.2	1986.1	2443.9	1507.0	1733.7	2065.6
Conservation and Development	3743.4	4274.7	4984.5	1089.7	1254.9	1442.9
Per Capita Output	19542.7	20111.9	20671.0	8890.7	11283.6	11981.6
Per capita public capital stock	2567.7	2425.1	2919.0	500.6	496.6	546.4
Per capita private capital stock	3043.1	3136.2	4054.4	2427.1	2399.7	2540.5

As Table 4 also indicates, total state and county public infrastructure capital stock grew by 34 percent while private capital stock increased 65 percent between 1982 and 1992. The ratio of state and county public capital to private capital showed a decline between these same periods. Approximately two thirds of this public capital is state-owned.

The production function was estimated using a translog production function and using the iterated seemingly unrelated regression (ITSUR) technique.[21] The parameter estimates for

[20] The study makes use of total public capital which includes such things as public school buildings and the like rather than the ċore infrastructure'since the results of their estimates are similar.

county-level production functions for 1992 and their t-statistics in parentheses are displayed in Table 5.[22] Variables are entered in the translog production function as deviations from their means to control for unobserved but state-specific fixed effects.[23] In the later part of this exercise, we will use a first difference form that would yet control for county level fixed-effects.

Column (1) shows the basic production function estimates without public capital. The input elasticities closely approximate the observed income shares. The positive coefficients of the squared terms in the private inputs offer evidence of either increasing returns in the private inputs or the fact that some counties are at different production possibility curves.

---

[21] The ITSUR method appears to fit the data better than the other estimation techniques. The iterated three stage least square method (IT3SLS) estimation technique was used in preliminary computation with intergovernmental finances (an important source of financing for local public expenditures) and population densities as instruments for possible endogeneity, but the results were sensitive to the construction of the instruments and they were volatile and less robust to specification changes than those based on ITSUR methods. Because of time and space, it was not possible to provide all the detailed results for each regression. However, I would gladly provide this information upon request.

[22] The results for 1982 and 1987 are not shown since they have somewhat similar results as 1992, and the fact that 1982 was the benchmark year makes 1992 less sensitive to any problems that can arise in developing a benchmark.

[23] To calculate county cross-sectional means, all the counties in a state under the study were considered as forming respective þseudo-states." For example, even though Alabama itself has about 67 counties, under the study it has only 48 counties. Therefore, to calculate its mean, we total the value of the variables in log and cross-logs forms for the 48 counties under the study and divide them by 48. This is the mean that is used to control for the fixed effects of the counties within each state.

Table 5
Regression Results: Translog Intercounty Production Function with Fixed Effects
Dependent Variable: Gross County Product (ln Q)[a]

Independent Variables: **The t-values of the coefficients (in absolute terms) are in parentheses.**	**Model Parameters**	**(1)** Basic equation	**(2)** **Basic equation with public capital input**	**(3)** **Basic equation with public capital input and regional effects**	**(4)** **Basic equation with public capital input and demographic effects**	**(5)** **Basic equation with public capital input in First difference form**[b]	**(6)** **Basic equation with public capital input in Pooled Regression form**[c]
intercept	β_o	6.03(3210.06)	6.03(3557.94)	6.04(2107.97)	6.03(1513.78)	0.076(20.93)	5.93(2402.39)
$\ln L - mean \ln L$	β_L	0.186(349.17)	0.186(364.60)	0.186(366.90)	0.186(368.94)	.156(15.33)	.192(390.78)
$\ln K - mean \ln K$	β_K	0.216(195.19	0.216(198.94)	0.216(198.8)	0.216(198.89)	0.211(13.74)	0.206(220.75)
$\ln M - mean \ln M$	β_M	0.598	0.598	0.598	0.599	0.633	0.602
$\ln G - mean \ln G$	β_G		0.023(9.90)	0.022(9.49)	0.024(9.39)	0.133(5.15)	-0.005(2.05)
$(\ln L)^2$-mean $(\ln L)^2$	β_{LL}	0.111(133.11)	0.113(130.06)	0.114(130.11)	0.114(131.27)	0.087(28.57)	0.095(89.27)
$(\ln K)^2$-mean $(\ln K)^2$	β_{KK}	0.094(102.23)	0.097(103.07)	0.097(102.86)	0.097(102.48)	0.107(22.34)	0.079(96.14)
$(\ln M)^2$-mean $(\ln M)^2$	β_{MM}	0.133	0.140	0.140	0.141	0.147	0.124
$(\ln G)^2$-mean $(\ln G)^2$	β_{GG}		-0.001(1.05)	-0.001(1.07)	-0.001(1.13)	0.002(0.24)	0.003(4.65)
$\ln K \ \ln L - mean \ln K \ \ln L$	β_{LK}	-0.036(50.71)	-0.035(49.46)	-0.035(49.46)	-0.035(49.28)	-0.023(9.58)	-0.025(36.41)
$\ln M \ \ln L - mean \ln M \ \ln L$	β_{LM}	-0.075	-0.078	-0.078	-0.079	-0.063	-0.070
$\ln G \ \ln L - mean \ln G \ \ln L$	β_{GL}		0.004(11.32)	0.004(11.19)	0.004(11.12)	-0.001(4.94)	-0.003(11.35)

Continued		**(1)**	**(2)**	**(3)**	**(4)**	**(5)**	**(6)**
$\ln K \ln M - mean \ln K \ln M$	β_{KM}	-0.058	-0.062	-0.062	-0.062	-0.084	-0.054
$(\ln K \ln G - mean \ln K \ln G)$	β_{KG}		0.005(10.68)	0.005(10.60)	0.005(10.57)	0.069(24.43)	0.0(0.41)
$(\ln G \ln M - mean \ln G \ln M)$	β_{GM}		0.009	-0.009	-0.009	-0.067	-0.004
Intercept for share of Labor	β_{TL}					-0.004(4.61)	
Intercept for share of Capital	β_{TK}					0.005(2.01)	
Dummy for 1982	β_{82}						0.017(5.55)
Dummy for 1987	β_{87}						-0.009(3.13)
Shadow price of Public capital	Z_G		0.410	0.399	0.421	0.410	0.045
Shadow price of Private capital	Z_K	1.052	1.031	1.031	1.03	1.031	0.891
Marginal Cost (MC)	Z_Q	1.310	1.312	1.225	1.217	1.13	1.29
Government's share	$S_G^* = \frac{\partial \ln Q^*}{\partial \ln G}$		0.023	0.022	0.024	0.133	-0.005
Labor's Share	$S_L^* = \frac{\partial \ln Q^*}{\partial \ln L}$	0.184	0.184	0.184	0.184	0.184	0.192
Capital's Share	$S_K^* = \frac{\partial \ln Q^*}{\partial \ln K}$	0.209	0.209	0.209	0.209	0.209	0.206

Continued		(1)	(2)	(3)	(4)	(5)	(6)
Cross Elasticity between Capital and Labor	$\eta_{KL} = \frac{\partial \ln L}{\partial \ln K}$	0.405	0.399	0.399	0.399	0.334	0.336
Cross Elasticity between Public capital and Labor	$\eta_{GL} = \frac{\partial \ln L}{\partial \ln G}$		0.001	0.0	0.002	0.138	-0.021
Cross Elasticity between Public capital and private Capital	$\eta_{KG} = \frac{\partial \ln K}{\partial \ln G}$		-0.0010	-0.002	-0.001	-0.197	-0.005
Regional effects considered		NO	NO	YES	NO	NO	NO
Demographic effects considered		NO	NO	NO	YES	NO	NO
Number of Observations		1514	1514	1514	1514	1342	4401
Adjusted R^2		0.998	0.998	0.998	0.998	0.840	0.995
Durbin Watson		1.868	1.9	1.9	1.9	1.96	1.6

a- The estimation results reported at the cross sectional level are for the census year 1992.

b- The first difference is taken between the two census years --1987 and 1992.

c- The pooled regression has used the three census years of the study--1982, 1987, 1992.

Column (2) adds infrastructure to the production function. The private input elasticities remain the same. The estimated elasticity of public capital on private sector production for counties is positive for all the cases (the cross-section (cols. 2 through 4), first difference (column 5) and pooled regression analysis (column 6)). However, except the first difference which show an estimated elasticity of 0.133, this value is a little more than 0.02 for the other equations and thus there is little evidence shown for a special role of public capital in affecting output or productivity. The negative coefficient of the squared term in infrastructure in the cross-section forms is an indication that public capital exhibited diminishing returns.

One possible explanation for the non-significant role of public capital just might be a weak relationship between infrastructure and output. A Pearson correlation analysis shows that even though public capital and output are highly correlated (80%), the amount of infrastructure does not seem to rise with per capita income (14%). It is generally believed that infrastructure is a normal good. Wealthy counties will then have more infrastructure while the poor ones will have less, but the differences are not large. This may explain the peripheral role played by infrastructure on private sector productivity and output at both the state and county levels.

Column (3) adds regional dummies to control for regional amenities.[24] Holtz-Eakin (1994) demonstrates the importance of controlling for unobserved heterogeneity among states and introduces a state-specific intercept into his estimation equation. In a similar fashion, we divided the states and counties into broad based regions of north, south, east, and west to capture any effects that comes of natural endowments. Regional differences did not reveal any additional information since regional dummies do not appear to add more information than removing state means or fixed-effects from the included regressors. The other parameters are largely unchanged.

Column (4) replaces regional dummies with Beale's codes in order to examine the possible existence of productivity differences in manufacturing due to the degree of urbanization. Counties are stratified into ten demographic groups: four metropolitan counties with population sizes of over 1 million to fewer than 250,000; 3 adjacent and 3 nonadjacent to a metro with population of over 20,000 to fewer than 2,500. Because the estimation is done using deviations from their means to control for state-specific effects, there is little or no change to the parameters indicating that there is no distinct pattern that comes from urbanization at the county level.

Column (5) shows the estimates from the first difference form. This form controls for correlation between unobserved county level fixed effects and output which may appear as a spurious correlation

---

[24] See Holtz-Eakin, Newey, and Rosen (1988) and Tatom (1991) for details.

between public capital and output. The first difference form is a more stringent test than the state level fixed-effects whose controls are somewhat limited. The first difference form may pick up more information about each counties characteristics than state level fixed effects.

The results of the regression in first difference form showed a positive coefficient for public capital. This implies an output elasticity of 0.133, a substantial effect. These results are not surprising when we consider the fact that only census years 1982, 1987, and 1992 are used as a first difference. A new highway system, for example, that was added five or ten years ago (i.e. in 1982 and 1987) would surely add to the states or counties output in five or ten years (1987 or 1992).

Holtz-Eakin (1994) uses a year-to-year variation in his first difference form which may be influenced by unobserved business cycle effects. This might explain why his first difference form estimate did not identify the role played by infrastructure at the state and regional levels. Over the longer periods used in this study, business cycles are minimized. Griliches and Hausman (1986) have suggested taking long period differences in order to reveal important relationships among variables considered without a simultaneity measurement bias.

One other possible explanation for the significant role of public capital for counties in first difference form may be that although measurement errors are present in the data, they are approximately of equal amount over time. Even though capital stock data is more appropriate than investment data, many assumptions and interpolations were needed and the capital stock data may in general contain substantial measurement error. The state values used in this study were reconciled to the national totals, but the county values were not adjusted to the state totals since the counties under study do not comprise the entire state. Thus the cross-county data is expected to pick up more noise than the cross-state data. Taking first differences would then eliminate or reduce the errors in the data and biases in the estimates drastically. However, it might also be the case that county level fixed-effects which was done using first difference forms picked up more information about each counties characteristics than the state level fixed-effects.

Pooling cross-section and time-series data of the three census years, column (6), offers more degrees of freedom for hypothesis testing and also introduces a time-series element for testing the applicability of the specified model throughout the counties. Cross-county parameter estimates reflect inter-county averages and thus are not applicable to each sample county. The pooled cross section specification enables us to stress the cross-section variation while controlling for the time variations. If counties with more public capital one year than the previous have more output during the year with more public capital, it is a clear indication that increasing public capital will increase output and income. To take account of the time dependent technological change, we incorporate yearly dummy variables for 1982 and 1987.

This specification allows the contribution of public capital to private sector output and productivity to differ across counties and across time.

In the pooled regression for counties, public capital plays an insignificant role in the private sector's economic performance. The public capital coefficient from the pooled data for counties is zero or negative. Even though time-series data is an important requirement to find the contribution of public capital to private sector productivity, the fact that 1982 was the benchmark year makes the combined data of 1982, 1987, and 1992 very sensitive to measurement errors. If that is the case, then the pooled regression results may not provide us with a clear indication of the relationship between infrastructure capital and output.

To allow us to conduct county and state analysis of the impact of public capital and private sector productivity and to investigate the possibility of more spillovers for larger units of analysis, we conduct a similar estimation at the state level. The parameter estimates and their t-statistics in parentheses for the various cross-state equation results are displayed in Table 6. Because the Beale's codes for U. S. counties pertain only to counties, this model is dropped. The results of the estimates across the states show elasticities of output that closely approximate income shares. While its magnitude and statistical significance varies, a positive infrastructure effect at the state level remains unchanged regardless of the modification done to the model.

Comparing county and state estimation results of Table 5 and Table 6, the evidence seems to suggest that the estimated coefficient on public capital rises with the level of aggregation. As indicated in all the cases (by the coefficient and output elasticity of public capital), the positive association between public capital and state output is consistently larger than the positive association between public capital and county output. The difference in findings may be due to the fact that using county data sets, one misses a fraction of the spillover benefit from the public capital stock.

Table 6

Regression Results: Translog Interstate Production Function with Fixed Effects Dependent Variable: Gross State Product (ln Q)[a]

Independent Variables: **The t-values of the coefficients (in absolute terms) are in parentheses.**	**Model Parameters**	**(1)** **Basic equation**	**(2)** **Basic equation with public capital input**	**(3)** **Basic equation with public capital input and regional effects**	**(5)** **Basic equation with public capital input in First difference form[b]**	**(6)** **Basic equation with public capital input in Pooled regression form[c]**
intercept	β_o	10.35(432.16)	10.37(480.0)	10.42(408.81)	-0.01(0.99)	10.33(2095.03)
$\ln L - mean \ln L$	β_L	0.180(92.95)	0.179(93.45)	0.178(107.16)	0.125(2.04)	0.181(97.30)
$\ln K - mean \ln K$	β_K	0.245(23.79)	0.238(24.21)	0.237(24.55)	0.094(0.55)	0.191(66.24)
$\ln M - mean \ln M$	β_M	0.573	0.584	0.585	0.781	0.629
$\ln G - mean \ln G$	β_G		0.0314(4.83)	0.042(5.18)	0.325(3.17)	0.074(1.81)
$(\text{Ln L})^2$-mean $(\ln \text{L})^2$	β_{LL}	0.144(55.27)	0.144(49.88)	0.140(51.38)	0.032(1.81)	0.084(21.59)
$(\text{Ln K})^2$-mean $(\ln \text{K})^2$	β_{KK}	0.337(23.03)	0.278(13.99)	0.284(14.51)	0.035(1.35)	0.072(24.08)
$(\text{Ln M})^2$-mean $(\ln \text{M})^2$	β_{MM}	0.484	0.403	0.405	0.035	0.109
$(\text{Ln G})^2$-mean $(\ln \text{G})^2$	β_{GG}		0.006(0.69)	0.008(0.92)	0.078(1.03)	-0.007(1.37)
$\ln K \ \ln L - mean \ln K \ \ln L$	β_{LK}	0.002(0.47)	-0.01(2.18)	-0.01(2.51)	-0.016(0.88)	-0.024(8.19)
$\ln M \ \ln L - mean \ln M \ \ln L$	β_{LM}	-0.145	-0.135	-0.131	-0.02	-0.061

Continued		(1)	(2)	(3)	(5)	(6)
$\ln G \ln L - mean \ln G \ln L$	β_{GL}		0.002(1.58)	-0.0001(0.08)	-0.001(1.26)	0.006(6.53)
$\ln K \ln M - mean \ln K \ln M$	β_{KM}	-0.339	-0.269	-0.275	-0.019	-0.049
$\ln K \ln G - mean \ln K \ln G$	β_{KG}		0.011(3.70)	0.007(2.14)	-0.01(0.33)	0.003(2.37)
$\ln G \ln M - mean \ln G \ln M$	β_{GM}		-0.012	-0.007	-0.01	-0.009
Intercept for share of Labor	β_{TL}				-0.003(1.36)	
Intercept for share of Capital	β_{TK}				0.013(1.01)	
Dummy for 1982	β_{82}					-0.024(3.82)
Dummy for 1987	β_{87}					-0.002(0.40)
Shadow price of Public capital	Z_G		0.563	0.653	0.563	0.695
Shadow price of Private capital	Z_K	.997	.992	1.02	.992	0.863
Marginal Cost (MC)	Z_Q	0.989	1.120	0.999	1.120	1.0
Government's share	$S_G^* = \frac{\partial \ln Q^*}{\partial \ln G}$		0.057	0.067	0.057	0.074
Labor's Share	$S_L^* = \frac{\partial \ln Q^*}{\partial \ln L}$	0.177	0.177	0.177	0.177	0.177
Capital's Share	$S_K^* = \frac{\partial \ln Q^*}{\partial \ln K}$	0.231	0.231	0.231	0.231	0.189

Continued		(1)	(2)	(3)	(5)	(6)
Cross Elasticity between Capital and Labor	$\eta_{KL} = \frac{\partial \ln L}{\partial \ln K}$	0.220	0.287	0.288	0.321	0.322
Cross Elasticity between Public capital and Labor	$\eta_{GL} = \frac{\partial \ln L}{\partial \ln G}$		0.046	0.068	0.060	0.041
Cross Elasticity between Public capital and private Capital	$\eta_{KG} = \frac{\partial \ln K}{\partial \ln G}$		0.01	0.037	0.11	0.058
Regional effects considered		NO	NO	YES	NO	NO
Demographic effects considered		NO	NO	NO	NO	NO
Number of Observations		50	50	50	50	150
Adjusted R^2		0.978	0.985	0.984	.951	0.999
Durbin Watson		2.08	1.93	2.01	1.75	1.5

a. The estimation results reported at the cross sectional level are for the census year 1992.

b. The first difference is taken between the two census years --1987 and 1992.

c. The pooled regression has used the three census years of the study--1982, 1987, 1992.

The county-level estimates may understate the overall impact of public capital since they cannot capture overlapping effects that come from the higher levels of public capital (i.e., from state and national), while estimates using state level data show somewhat a greater role for public sector capital than county levels.[25]

Moreover, the ratio of per capita public to private capital is much larger for the states than for the counties (84% vs. 21% in 1982). The counties under study also accounted for at least 85% to 90% of the private capital in the state's manufacturing sector, while these same counties accounted for a little over more than half of the total state's public capital stock. States are then in a position to capture benefits of infrastructure more completely than counties as well as better positioned than counties to choose feasible projects.[26]

The spillover elasticity of public capital on private sector output is positive and statistically significant in all the cases except the spillover elasticity for the pooled county data that showed a negative or roughly zero value. Based on the cross-sectional, pooled and first difference regressions, the results also show consistently that public capital explain a larger portion of private sector output and productivity at the state level than at the county level. This difference may be that aggregation does affect infrastructure effects because states capture additional spillover.

Among the studies that report a positive public infrastructure contribution to the private sector economy, one of the few consistent findings may be that these estimates increase with the level of aggregation. Table 7 summarizes some of the empirical studies done by level of aggregation with positive infrastructure contribution to the private sector economy.

The fact that the shadow price of public capital, Z_G, implies a higher level of return at the state level than at the county level in all the cases partly also confirms that the higher the aggregation the higher the spillover. However, when you carefully control for other things, the study finds that public

[25] A regressor could be introduced in each of the equations that averages the public capital in adjacent counties (for the over 1500 counties) and see whether it has a positive and statistically significant coefficient estimate to test if there is a larger public capital spillover with higher level of aggregation. However, this test could not be performed in this case because some adjacent counties are not in the study.

[26] This result is consistent with some past findings such as Munnell (1992) that showed that the coefficients of public capital would rise with the level of aggregation (where it was shown that regional data having a greater role of public capital than state data). Munnell (1992) reports that her past and present findings of public infrastructure capital had a positive impact on output at the state level, although the output elasticity was roughly half the size of her national estimate (0.34 vs. 0.15). Munnell argues that spillover effects increase with the level of aggregation. The intuitive argument of positive externalities is that at the less aggregated level one misses a fraction of the spillover benefits from public capital. Based on Munnellš estimate above, the output elasticity of infrastructure of 0.19 (the difference between national and state values) is the out-of-state spillovers that are not captured by the state making the investment. Similarly, this study found a larger out-of-county spillovers benefit than for the county making the investment.

infrastructure does have a small impact on output and productivity at both the state and county levels, but that its influence is relegated to a peripheral role.

Moreover, the elasticity of output with respect to public capital, S_G, which helps us understand infrastructure's contribution to private sector productivity is 0.02 regardless of what model is chosen at the county level, while it is at least 0.06 at the state level. Consequently, public capital's contribution to private sector productivity $\left(S_G \frac{\dot{G}}{G}\right)$ at the county level is merely six-hundredth of a percent, while public capital's contribution to private sector productivity at the state level is two-tenth of a percent.

In general, parameter estimates for private inputs were robust to changes in specification such as introducing regional and demographic dummies, first difference, and pooling the data of the three census years, and the estimated parameters are of correct signs, and of reasonable magnitude for state and county level analysis. The resulting high R^2 (0.95 and higher in all the cases except for the county level first difference form which registered an R^2 of 0.84) in all the regressions provide a reasonable fit of the sample. Moreover, the equations look sensible, with private input coefficients almost equal to their shares of total income at both the state and county levels. When we consider the fact that common variables together with infrastructure capital were able to explain a greater portion of output and productivity, the model has performed adequately.

The negative cross effects among all the private inputs and between materials and public capital in all the columns for the counties as well as the states indicate that they are substitutes, while labor and private capital show positive and statistically significant cross effects with public capital and thus they are complementarity at the county level and no effects at the state level. The complementarity between labor and public capital as well as private and public capital could imply that public capital enhances the operation of private capital, while the substitutability of public capital and intermediate inputs indicate that public capital stock can directly affect economic activity by reducing the need for some intermediates in private sector firms.

Table 7

A Selective Survey on the Estimates of Public Sector Elasticity on Private sector Output According to level of aggregation

Name	*Level of Aggregation*	*Elasticity of Public capital*	*dependent Variables used*	*Comments*
D. Aschauer (1989)	national	0.39	private Business output	time-series, (1949-1985), Cobb-Douglas
A. Munnell (1990a)	national	0.33	Nonagricultural output	time-series, (1949-1987), Cobb-Douglas
Costa, Ellson, Martin (1987)	state	0.20	manufacturing state output	cross-section, 1972, Translog function
A. Munnell (1990b) *	state	0.15	Nonagricultural state output	pooled, (1970-1986), Cobb-Douglas
A. Munnell (1990b)**	state	0.06	Nonagricultural state output	pooled, (1970-1986), Cobb-Douglas
K. T. Duffy-Deno & R. W. Eberts (1989) *	28 SMSAs	0.08	personal income	pooled; (1980-1984); log form
R. W. Eberts (1986)	38 SMSAs	0.03	manufacturing state output	time-series, (1958-1981), translog

* - estimated under no constraint in technology

** - estimated under constant returns to scale technology in the private inputs.

*** - the authors did not estimate a production function, but instead used per capita personal income as the dependent variable.

With similar past findings mixed, these results are not totally inconsistent. Hulten and Schwab (1993), for example, found that private inputs (capital and labor) are the most important sources of regional manufacturing differential in growth rates and not public capital. However, they suggested that public capital may have played an essential role in facilitating the movement of the private inputs. Eberts (1986) finds public capital and labor to be substitutes, while Deno (1988) finds complementarity between the same two inputs. Dalenberg (1987) found that at the regional level public capital and labor are weak complements while public capital, energy and private capital are substitutes.

The negative cross effects among all the private inputs and between materials and public capital in all the columns for the counties as well as the states indicate that they are substitutes, while labor and private capital show positive and statistically significant cross effects with public capital and thus they are complementarity at the county level and no effects at the state level. The complementarity between labor and public capital as well as private and public capital could imply that public capital enhances the operation of private capital,[27] while the substitutability of public capital and intermediate inputs indicate that public capital stock can directly affect economic activity by reducing the need for some intermediates in private sector firms. With similar past findings mixed, these results are not totally inconsistent. For example, Eberts (1986) finds public capital and labor to be substitutes, while Deno (1988) finds complementarity between the same two inputs. Dalenberg (1987) found that at the regional level public capital and labor are weak complements while public capital, energy and private capital are substitutes.

Furthermore, the effect of public capital on the demand for private capital and labor as exemplified by the cross elasticity between public capital and labor (respectively, η_{KG} and η_{GL}) at the state level is at least 4 percent for labor and at least 1 percent for private capital, while this same value is zero or negative at the county level (except for the first difference form which registered a 13.8 percent effect of public capital in the demand for labor).

In the next part of the exercise, the study will address the issue of productivity performance and productivity convergence between the older well developed U. S. counties and the recently developed counties as well as the role played by public infrastructure.

---

[27] Hulten and Schwab (1993), for example, found that private inputs (capital and labor) are the most important sources of regional manufacturing differential in growth rates and not public capital. However, they suggested that public capital may have played an essential role in facilitating the movement of the private inputs.

V. Productivity Performance and Productivity Convergence Across U. S. Counties

County level data allows us to address the issue of productivity convergence. This implicitly tests the assertion that the older areas (with so-called deteriorating infrastructure and aging capital stock) may have suffered in productivity growth relative to smaller more recently developed areas of the U. S.[28] Given that the U. S. has relatively homogeneous technology and work ethics, the county level analysis is then a promising source of information on productivity growth and productivity convergence (compared to comparative studies done of different nations with different institutional arrangements such as cultural heritage, political stability, etc.).

Productivity convergence may occur by increasing capital intensity or attaining similar levels of technology. Labor productivity (measures output/hour) does not allow the separate identification in the influence of capital and technology, while the neoclassical growth framework places heavy emphasis on accumulation of capital as the driving force behind convergence. Therefore, to compare productivity across counties, it is important to consider both labor and multifactor productivity measures.[29]

Labor Productivity change is modelled as a function of earlier levels of labor productivity:

$$\Delta \ln\left(\frac{Y}{L}\right)_i = \alpha + \beta \ln\left(\frac{Y}{L}\right)_i^{base,yr} \tag{10}$$

The equation used to estimate multifactor Productivity (MFP) change is similar:

$$\Delta \ln MFP_i = \alpha + \beta \ln MFP_i^{base,yr} \tag{11}$$

where i stands for the ith state or county and where the speed of convergence, λ, for both measures is calculated from the following equation:

$$\beta = \frac{1-(1-\lambda)^T}{T} \tag{12}$$

The speed of convergence can be interpreted as the rate at which productivity is converging to some U. S. average productivity level. The basic convergence results for labor productivity and multifactor productivity measures is shown on Table 8 below.

---

[28] See, for example, Carlino (1985) and Carlino and Mills (1987). Studies have found the Rural Renaissance"may have resulted not only in the north losing to the south and west but also to their own hinterland.

[29] See Bernard, Andrew B., and Charles I. Jones (1996) where these points are further expanded and statistically measured.

Table 8

Convergence regressions: Labor Productivity (LP)

and Multifactor Productivity (MFP)

Regions	**β (t-value)**	**λ**	**Adjusted R^2**
LP-State	-0.0625 (7.07)	0.0559	0.51
LP-County	-0.0081 (23.52)	0.0080	0.30
MFP-State	-0.1507 (12.19)	0.1189	0.76
MFP-County	-0.0152 (427.10)	0.0148	0.99

The coefficients (β) on initial productivity levels are negative and significant for both labor and multifactor productivity across states and counties. This indicates that lagging states and counties are catching up to the most productive states and counties in the U. S. However, there is evidence for faster convergence in multifactor productivity measure than in labor productivity measure. This may suggest that more productive counties are able to offset some of the gains in MFP through relatively greater capital investment.

This finding is somewhat in direct contrast to international studies done on productivity convergence which find very limited or even non-convergence among the most productive compared to the least productive countries. For example, in accounting for differences in output per worker across countries, where their finding showed an output per worker 48 times higher in the most productive compared to the least productive countries in 1988, Hall and Jones (1996) conclude that differences in governmental, cultural and natural infrastructure are the main contributors to this variation. However, for the U. S. states and counties where we have an established private property rights, openness to trade, common language and a temperate climate, it would not be surprising for the least productive to catch up with the most productive states and counties.

Furthermore, looking at the speed of convergence (λ) which determines how fast the less productive counties catch up with the more productive ones, the state results show relatively rapid convergence compared to county results. About 5.6 percent of the gap is closed in five years for the states compared to only 0.8 percent for the counties. The corresponding figures for multifactor productivity are 11.9 percent for the states versus 1.5 percent for the counties. This might be indirect evidence of why infrastructure plays a larger role at the state level than at the county level since the speed of convergence could be affected by spillover effects that come about from aggregation. This could be one of the explanations as to why the results show the private economy responding more to state level infrastructure than at the county level.

VI. Summary and Conclusion

Public infrastructure capital was incorporated as an additional input into a production function to analyze its impact on private sector productivity at the county level. The county level is chosen as a unit of analysis in order to minimize the impact of the macro-economy on the estimates. Counties are the smallest geographical areas for which significant amounts of data are available. Because output is less correlated across counties than across states or regions and at the county level, national influences are considerably muted and the correlation between county level output growth and national growth are weaker, analyses of infrastructure at the county level are more likely to measure the impact of infrastructure on output.

The attempt to measure the impact of public infrastructure capital on private sector productivity in various parts of the country is made possible by the development of private and public capital stock at the state and, especially, at the county level. We constructed a measure of private and public capital stocks based on the perpetual inventory technique for a sample of a little over 1500 counties within the 50 U. S. states. The data is an effort to create a complete set of national accounts at the state and county levels for inputs, outputs and public infrastructure at any level of industry in the hope of allocating U. S. economic growth to its sources at local levels.

The next step was to determine if the county and state data can offer more direct evidence on the impact of public capital on the growth of private sector output, productivity, and employment. We used these data to estimate a translog production function to see if the positive relationship between output and public capital (which has been documented at the national, regional, state, and SMSA levels) holds up for county level analysis. The present study is based on a larger and broader sample that is largely devoid of macro-economic influences than previous studies done on the topic.

The estimation of the system of equations for a large sample of counties suggests that the model has great promise for evaluating infrastructure effects on the private sector economy. The explanatory power of the cross-sectional, pooled and first difference regression are high with an R^2 of over 0.95 at both the state and local levels, except for the first difference form at the county level with an R^2 of over 0.84.

By and large, the results of the study are mixed and thus suggestive but hardly conclusive. The spillover elasticity of public capital on private sector output is small but positive and statistically significant in all cases at both the state and local levels, except when data are pooled for the three census years. The spillover elasticity for counties in this case is negative or roughly zero. The results also show that the spillover elasticity for states is consistently larger than the county data. This difference may be due to states capturing cross county spillover. Because the translog estimation is done using deviations from their means to control for unobserved county specific effects, state-level and county-level estimates show no regional productivity differences and nor differences by levels of urbanization.

The study also examines productivity performance and productivity convergence across states and counties. Productivity convergence may occur by increasing capital intensity or attaining similar levels of technology. This implicitly tests the assertion that the older counties with aging capital stock may have suffered in productivity growth relative to smaller more recently developed counties of the U. S. The estimates show that while convergence is slow, it is occurring faster at the state level than at the county level, which has a similar implication of spillovers increasing with the level of aggregation.

The results suggest that much could be learned by examining the public infrastructure-private output relationship from a large micro sample, especially for time series. In addition, public sector capital could be divided into different components of public capital such as highways, natural resources, utility, sanitation, sewerage system and education to determine the relative impacts of these various capital stocks on private sector productivity. It would also be interesting to consider intergovernmental fiscal relations, because decisions made at the federal and state levels of government may affect the incentive to invest (therefore the marginal product) in public infrastructure of the metropolitan and county levels of government. Counties and states exhibit a wide array of fiscal behaviors and economic growth patterns and the available samples should be large enough to produce reliable cross-county estimates.

REFERENCES

Aaron, Henry J. "Why is Infrastructure Important? Discussion" in Alicia H. Munnell, Is There a Shortfall in Public Capital Investment? ed.: Alicia H. Munnell, Conference series No. 34. Boston: Federal Reserve Bank of Boston, 1990, pp. 51-63.

Aschauer, David A. "Is Public Expenditure Productive?" J. Monetary Economics, 1989a, March, 23(2), pp.177-200.

_______. "Does Public Capital Crowd out Private Capital?" J. Monetary Economics, 1989b, March, 24(2), pp.171-188.

_______. " Why Is Infrastructure Important? in Alicia H. Munnell, Is There a Shortfall in Public Capital Investment? ed.: Alicia H. Munnell, Conference series No. 34. Boston: Federal Reserve Bank of Boston, 1990. pp. 21-50.

Baily, Martin N., Hulten, Charles R. and David Campbell. "Productivity Dynamics in Manufacturing Plants", Brookings Paper: Macroeconomics, 1992, pp. 187-267.

Bartelsman, Eric J., and Phoebus J. Dhrymes. "Productivity Dynamics: U. S. Manufacturing Plants, 1972-1986," Discussion paper Center for Economic Studies, Bureau of the Census, 1992, 6, February.

Basu, Susanto and John G. Fernald. "Returns to Scale in U. S. Production: Estimates and Implications," Journal of Political Economy, 1997, 105, pp. 249-283.

Beeson, Patricia E. "Productivity Growth and the Decline of Manufacturing in Large Metropolitan Areas: 1959-1978," Fed. Res. Bank of Cleveland Working Paper 1986, no. 8607, July.

Bernard, Andrew B., and Charles I. Jones. "Comparing Apples and Oranges: Productivity Convergence and Measurement Across Industries and Countries," The American Economic Review, 1996, December.

Boskin, Michael J., Marc S. Robinson and Alan M. Huber. "New Estimates of State and Local Government Tangible Capital and Net Investment," 1987, January, NBER working paper #2131.

Butler, Margaret. "Rural -Urban Continuum Codes for Metro and Non-metro Counties", Agriculture and Rural Economy Division, Economic Research Service, U. S. D. A., 1990, April, Staff report no. 9028.

Carlino, Gerald. "Declining City Productivity and the Growth of Rural Regions", Journal Of Urban Economics, 1985, 18, 11-27.

Carlton, Dennis W. "The Location and Employment Choices of New Firms: An Econometric Model with Discrete and Endogenous Variables", The Review of Economics and Statistics, 1983, 65, pp. 440-449.

Gerald A. Carlino and Edwin S. Mills. "The Determinant of County Growth", Journal of Regional Science, 1987, Vol.27, No. 1, (39-54).

Costa, Jose da Silva, Richard W. Ellson, and Randolph C. Martin. "Public Capital, Regional Output, and Development: Some Empirical Evidence," Journal of Regional Science, 1987, August, 27, 419-37.

Duffy-Deno, Kevin T. and Eberts, Randall W. "Public Infrastructure and Regional Economic Development: A Simultaneous Equations Approach," J. Urban Economics, 1991, November, 30(3), pp. 329-43.

Eberts, Randall W. "Estimating the Contribution of Urban Public Infrastructure to Regional Economic Growth," Fed. Res. Bank of Cleveland Working Paper, 1986, no. 8610, December.

Eisner, Robert. "Infrastructure and Regional Economic Performance: Comment," New England Economic Review, 1991, September/October, pp. 47-58.

Evans, Paul and Georgios Karras. " Are Governments Activities Productive? Evidence From A Panel of U. S. States," The Review of Economics and Statistics, 1994, February, 76(1), pp.1-11.

Fernald, John. "How Productive Is Infrastructure? Distinguishing Reality and Illusion with a Panel of U. S. Industries," Federal Reserve Board Discussion Paper, 1993, August.

Friedlaender, Ann F. "How Does Public Infrastructure Affect Regional Economic Performance? Discussion," in Alicia H. Munnell, Is There a Shortfall in Public Capital Investment? ed.: Alicia H. Munnell, Conference series No. 34. Boston: Federal Reserve Bank of Boston, 1990, pp. 108-12.

Gramlich, Edward M. "Infrastructure Investment: A Review Essay," Journal of Economic Literature, 1994, September, 32, pp. 1176-1196.

Griliches, Zvi, and Jerry A. Hausman. "Errors in variables in Panel Data," Journal of Econometrics, 1986, 31, 93-118.

Guilkey, David K., C. A. Knox lovell, and Robin Sickles. "A Comparison of the Performance of three Flexible Functional Forms," International Economic Review, 1983, 24 October, pp. 591-616.

Hall, Robert E., and Charles Jones. "The Productivity of Nations," NBER Working paper series, 1996, No. 5812, November.

Holtz-Eakin, Douglas. "Public Sector Capital and the Productivity Puzzle," The Review of Economics and Statistics, 1994, February, 76(1), pp. 12-21.

_________. "State-Specific Estimates of State and Local Government Capital," Regional Science and Urban Economics, 1993a, 23, pp. 185-209.

_________. "Public Investment in Infrastructure," Journal of Economic Perspectives, 1993b, November, 7, pp. 231-234.

Hulten, Charles R._and Robert M. Schwab. "Regional Productivity Growth in U. S. Manufacturing 1951-78", American Economic Review, 1984, 74 152-162.

Hulten, Charles R. and Robert M. Schwab. " Endogenous Growth, Public Capital, and the Convergence of Regional Manufacturing Industries," NBER Working paper series, 1993, No. 4538, November.

________ and ______. "Is there too Little Public Capital? Infrastructure and Public Growth," Paper Presented at the American Enterprise Institute Conference on Infrastructure Needs and Policy Options for the 1990s, Washington D. C., 1991, February 4.

Hulten, Charles R._and F. C. Wykoff. "The Measurement of Economic Depreciation," in C. R. Hulten, ed., Depreciation, Inflation, and the Taxation of Income from Capital, (Washington: Urban Institute), 1981, 81-125.

Jorgenson, Dale. "Fragile Statistical Foundations: The Macroeconomics of Public Infrastructure Investment," Comment on Hulten and Schwab (1991), Paper Presented at the American Enterprise Institute Conference on Infrastructure Needs and Policy Options for the 1990s, Washington D. C., 1991, February 4.

Kaizuka, K. "Public goods and decentralization of production", Review of Economics and Statistics, 1965, 30, 151-179.

Kevin T. Deno. "The Effect of Public Capital on U. S. Manufacturing Activity: 1970 to 1978," Southern Economic Journal, 1988, 55(2), pp.400-411.

McGuckin, Robert H._and Suzanne Peck. "Manufacturing Establishments Reclassified into New Industries: The Effects of Survey Design Rules," Discussion paper Center for Economic Studies, Bureau of the Census, 1992, November.

Mera, Koichi. "Regional Production Functions and Social Overhead Capital: An Analysis of the Japanese case," Regional and Urban Economics, 1973, May, 3, 157-85.

Munnell, Alicia H. "Why Has Productivity Growth Declined? Productivity and Public Investment," New England Economic Review, 1990a, January/February, pp. 3-22.

_________. "How Does Public Infrastructure Affect Regional Economic Performance?" in Alicia Munnell, Conference series No. 34. Boston: Federal Reserve Bank of Boston, 1990b, pp. 69-103.

_________. "Infrastructure Investment and Economic Growth," J. Economic Perspectives, 1992, Fall, 6(4), pp. 189-98.

Nadiri, Ishaq M._and Theofanis P. Mamuneas._"The Effects of Public Infrastructure and R & D Capital on the Cost Structure and Performance of U. S. Manufacturing Industries" The Review of Economics and Statistics, 1994, February, 76(1), pp. 22-37.

Schultz, Charles L. The politics and economics of Public spending, Brookings Institution, 1968..

Shah, Anwar. "Dynamics of Public Infrastructure Industrial Productivity and Profitability", The Review of Economics and Statistics, 1992, pp. 28-36.

Tatom, John A. "Public Capital and Private Sector Performance," Federal Reserve Bank of St. Louis Review, 1991, May/June, 73(3), pp. 3-15.

Tatom, John A. "The Spurious Effect of Public Capital Formation on Private Sector Productivity", Policy Studies Journal, 1993, Vol. 21, No.2, (391-395).

U. S. Bureau of the Census. County and City Data Book File, County Data 1947-1977, 1977, Washington, D. C.

Department of Commerce (DOC). "Fixed Reproducible Tangible Wealth in the United States: Revised Estimates for 1993-1995 and Summary Estimates for 1925-1996", Survey of Current Business, 1997, 9, page 37.

_________. "Improved Estimates of Fixed Reproducible Tangible Wealth, 1929-95", Survey of Current Business, 1997, 5, page 69.

_________. "The Measurement Description in the U. S. National Income and Product Account", 1997, 7, page 7.

APPENDIX Table 1

The Estimates of Private and Public State Capital stocks

(unit: Millions of 1992 dollars)

STATE NAMES	PRIVATE CAPITAL STOCK	PRIVATE CAPITAL STOCK	PRIVATE CAPITAL STOCK	PUBLIC CAPITAL STOCK	PUBLIC CAPITAL STOCK	PUBLIC CAPITAL STOCK
	1982	1987	1992	1982	1987	1992
ALABAMA	6747.5	7639.8	9671.3	3656.2	3913.4	4310.1
ALASKA	513.3	546.4	592.1	3855.1	4130.1	4227.4
ARIZONA	5644.9	6767.1	7803.4	3925.2	4625.9	5478.2
ARKANSAS	5225.9	5568.6	6069.1	1456.5	1642.4	1874.5
CALIFORNIA	67334.5	70663.3	72977.6	18774.2	21459.5	25617.9
COLORADO	5700.4	6493.7	7122.1	3295.5	3829.6	4583.3
CONNECTICUT	9203.4	9569.9	10034.4	2089.8	2421	3022.3
DELAWARE	832.2	879.7	969.2	218.9	626.9	950.6
FLORIDA	13147.5	14362.3	14813.2	12119.7	13808.6	16115.4
GEORGIA	14148.4	16349.6	18705.2	5832.9	6646.2	7657.8
HAWAII	1422.9	1580.8	2005	634.3	676.2	671.5
IDAHO	1224	1292.9	1712	911.1	991.9	1131.5
ILLINOIS	27855.6	29085.8	30934.3	10019.2	11082.8	12553.7
INDIANA	16382.6	18759.5	21849.6	4075.3	4427.7	5026.4
IOWA	10252.3	9677.5	10045.7	2985.4	3215.5	3562.1
KANSAS	5653.5	6236.7	6460.7	2386.7	2625.1	2967.1
KENTUCKY	10400.5	12107.7	13379.8	3246.5	3557.5	3956.9
LOUISIANA	4418.6	6562.6	8845.8	5749.7	6126.6	6440.8
MAINE	1512.2	1786.3	2033.5	873.1	963.7	1092.6
MARYLAND	6336.2	6600.9	7124.7	5700.8	6249.2	6789.4
MASSACHUSETTS	16291.2	16160	15852.6	3638.9	4209.7	5033.3
MICHIGAN	15248.6	19370.2	23151.5	6551.6	7112.8	7979.1
MINNESOTA	8294.2	9190.7	10263.2	5449.8	5974.5	6711.3
MISSISSIPPI	5327.5	5607.9	6239.9	2260.4	2417.7	2669.8
MISSOURI	14196.1	15220.9	15939.6	3502.3	3910.5	4493.7
MONTANA	957.3	1048.8	1164.8	107.3	280.8	434.5
NEBRASKA	3260.9	3176.6	3285.8	1786.6	1947	2139.6
NEVADA	612.3	671.6	725.8	1354.2	1495.9	1786.5
NEW HAMPSHIRE	3097.2	3009.3	2981.6	736.9	818.3	911.4
NEW JERSEY	18560.8	18845.1	19448.9	6708.5	7500.1	8622.2
NEW MEXICO	1546.5	1765.7	2218.6	2001.6	2184.8	2383
NEW YORK	43035.4	41961.7	41218.2	19533.5	21846.9	25087.1
NORTH CAROLINA	29237.6	32695.2	35004.9	3606.6	4220.1	5197.3
NORTH DAKOTA	1033.7	1096.1	1170.9	292.5	336.7	428.3
OHIO	31725.5	34345.8	37848.5	9193.1	9966.7	11164.1
OKLAHOMA	5880.7	6401.3	7003.1	3664.3	3939.7	4228.3
OREGON	4398.2	4721.3	5571.3	2657.5	2891.1	3256
PENNSYLVANIA	26814	27691.7	29541.7	7770.5	8553.2	9952.5
RHODE ISLAND	2403.7	2308.3	2186.8	649.8	707	821.5
SOUTH CAROLINA	8061.3	9371.9	11157.6	2007.8	2297.7	2778.3
SOUTH DAKOTA	979.4	934.9	955	774.8	889.3	1014.7
TENNESSEE	13273.8	14372.3	16789.5	3830.9	4269	4952
TEXAS	25282.4	28835.9	34226.6	17761.9	20130.1	22560.6
UTAH	2497.6	2773.2	3160.9	1787.5	2029.9	2278.8
VERMONT	1255.3	1484.5	1774.6	429.6	469.5	517.8
VIRGINIA	17925.5	19117.5	19980	4374.6	4921.4	5760.8
WASHINGTON	3944.5	5618.2	8861.5	6125.1	6798.5	7941.1
WEST VIRGINIA	2346.4	2696.1	3248	2030	2156.2	2281.2
WISCONSIN	16740.4	16978.3	18355.2	5595.9	5939.2	6513.2
WYOMING	1795.4	1892.4	1969	152.5	255.5	393.3

APPENDIX Table 2

The Estimates of Private and Public County Capital stocks
The 100 largest counties

(unit: Millions of 1992 dollars)

COUNTY NAMES	PRIVATE CAPITAL STOCK	PRIVATE CAPITAL STOCK	PRIVATE CAPITAL STOCK	PUBLIC CAPITAL STOCK	PUBLIC CAPITAL STOCK	PUBLIC CAPITAL STOCK
	1982	1987	1992	1982	1987	1992
LOS ANGELES COUNTY, CA	23949.6	23877.9	22779.0	3763.1	4177.1	4890.9
COOK COUNTY, IL	16483.5	15877.1	15742.5	3500.6	3837.1	4299.7
SANTA CLARA COUNTY, CA	11459.3	12979.3	14272.0	816.9	956.4	1139.9
MONROE COUNTY, NY	9931.2	9005.8	8204.8	608.4	651.0	709.1
NEW YORK CITY AREA	9263.6	8104.4	7587.9	6191.0	6851.3	8060.3
RICHMOND CITY AREA	7939.1	7911.2	7469.7	106.1	121.5	142.3
FORSYTH COUNTY, NC	7133.7	6725.1	5948.1	77.9	85.2	98.1
HAMILTON COUNTY, OH	7105.2	6948.5	7418.3	500.0	543.2	609.3
JEFFERSON COUNTY, KY	6588.1	6294.4	5829.8	122.8	146.5	199.9
ORANGE COUNTY, CA	6517.6	6671.8	6614.6	1050.8	1129.2	1349.6
DALLAS COUNTY, TX	5598.7	5667.1	5556.8	1170.7	1346.8	1641.3
MONTGOMERY COUNTY, PA	4744.7	4558.3	4748.6	221.2	240.9	260.6
ALAMEDA COUNTY, CA	4398.1	4493.6	5101.2	715.4	813.6	944.5
HARRIS COUNTY, TX	4343.0	5035.8	6126.4	2996.4	3280.7	3530.2
ESSEX COUNTY, MA	4237.1	3894.4	3650.5	273.7	298.2	326.7
MARICOPA COUNTY, AZ	4197.6	4811.2	5501.9	1658.2	1877.2	2210.8
MILWAUKEE COUNTY, WI	3893.2	3604.4	3577.8	908.7	996.2	1170.9
MIDDLESEX COUNTY, MA	3815.4	3982.1	3879.5	365.2	411.0	467.8
SUFFOLK COUNTY, NY	3420.5	3383.2	3125.0	536.2	600.7	679.0
SAN DIEGO COUNTY, CA	3344.0	3558.7	3794.0	1002.2	1116.1	1343.8
MARION COUNTY, IN	3284.0	3380.8	3924.0	478.8	525.1	592.3
CUYAHOGA COUNTY, OH	3275.8	2597.1	2408.8	864.1	933.9	1026.2
OAKLAND COUNTY, MI	3181.3	4057.2	4232.0	452.6	490.1	562.7
WAKE COUNTY, NC	3107.4	3443.1	3734.4	111.6	148.8	226.8
NASSAU COUNTY,NY	2899.3	2767.6	2468.2	1358.9	1442.7	1526.1
FRANKLIN COUNTY, OH	2822.8	2633.1	2617.7	443.9	486.0	588.5
MIDDLESEX COUNTY, NJ	2751.9	2854.1	2891.5	355.2	373.5	400.5
OKLAHOMA COUNTY, OK	2715.9	2841.4	2914.5	499.4	526.9	559.1
ST. LOUIS CITY AREA	2713.8	2786.1	2788.1	279.3	322.7	406.1
AIKEN COUNTY, SC	2692.9	2310.9	1965.1	28.6	31.8	36.7
GUILFORD COUNTY, NC	2597.0	2674.6	2763.8	129.7	141.4	165.0
ROCKLAND COUNTY, NY	2580.2	2284.0	1988.4	100.6	126.4	151.3
WAYNE COUNTY, MI	2557.2	4800.3	6705.1	1440.9	1526.9	1654.4
BIBB COUNTY, GA	2550.8	2376.2	2394.7	98.8	104.5	121.7
BALTIMORE CITY AREA	2499.7	2324.3	2266.8	1400.7	1453.8	1481.7
FULTON COUNTY, GA	2446.7	2695.3	2539.6	628.8	686.0	761.7
NEW HAVEN COUNTY, CT	2324.4	2424.0	2642.6	183.1	215.9	280.5
JACKSON COUNTY, MO	2303.2	2411.6	2618.1	455.9	503.1	602.5
ST. LOUIS COUNTY, MO	2258.3	2534.7	2614.6	267.8	289.5	328.0
HARTFORD COUNTY, CT	2170.4	2387.2	2587.3	305.3	346.7	419.7
DADE COUNTY, FL	2140.3	2041.3	1904.4	1920.8	2035.6	2164.5
BERGEN COUNTY, NJ	2129.1	2040.3	1960.0	321.0	341.7	368.9
FAIRFIELD COUNTY, CT	2070.3	2168.4	2236.1	345.9	392.2	454.9
PALM BEACH COUNTY, FL	2034.4	2020.6	1925.3	691.6	768.0	907.2
KENT COUNTY, MI	2026.6	2354.5	2679.8	133.0	152.8	196.8
ERIE COUNTY, NY	1993.0	2220.0	2424.7	928.0	959.0	974.2
WORCESTER COUNTY, MA	1936.1	1874.1	1874.5	263.7	291.8	315.5

COUNTY NAMES	PRIVATE CAPITAL	PRIVATE CAPITAL	PRIVATE CAPITAL	PUBLIC CAPITAL	PUBLIC CAPITAL	PUBLIC CAPITAL
Continued	**1982**	**1987**	**1992**	**1982**	**1987**	**1992**
VENTURA COUNTY, CA	1884.8	1938.8	2072.0	337.5	366.4	412.0
LINN COUNTY, IA	1820.5	1665.3	1633.9	101.5	110.4	125.0
LANCASTER COUNTY, PA	1808.9	1963.5	2142.6	109.1	122.2	156.4
SAN MATEO COUNTY	1807.4	1815.6	1965.2	266.3	294.5	346.7
CLAY COUNTY, MO	1790.0	1901.8	1899.1	49.9	54.9	63.5
WAUKESHA COUNTY, WI	1742.7	1794.2	1913.5	161.7	173.6	199.7
HENNEPIN COUNTY, MN	1708.2	2086.9	2372.4	688.9	756.2	894.7
ESSEX COUNTY, NJ	1661.3	1903.9	2233.5	331.7	352.1	396.5
TRAVIS COUNTY, TX	1632.5	2034.7	2787.5	345.3	428.2	519.5
LORAIN COUNTY, OH	1631.8	1538.2	1599.5	58.1	67.4	83.0
ROCKINGHAM COUNTY, NC	1596.9	1507.6	1486.3	14.5	17.2	21.5
UNION COUNTY, NJ	1529.4	1529.0	1553.5	170.7	186.6	216.2
PROVIDENCE COUNTY, RI	1519.7	1470.9	1306.4	221.5	225.4	230.1
ARAPAHOE COUNTY, CO	1508.0	1508.5	1721.6	329.9	389.2	459.6
BALTIMORE COUNTY, MD	1471.2	1615.6	1486.0	365.1	391.8	432.1
MORRIS COUNTY, NJ	1466.5	1678.8	2033.2	250.1	263.3	290.7
PASSAIC COUNTY, NJ	1464.9	1447.3	1422.8	209.8	216.8	228.0
DUVAL COUNTY, FL	1437.0	1376.1	1430.5	357.9	393.7	448.2
HUDSON COUNTY, NJ	1436.2	1387.5	1226.9	212.8	238.2	261.6
SUFFOLK COUNTY, MA	1433.6	1402.7	1390.3	210.1	245.3	315.4
SALT LAKE COUNTY, UT	1426.9	1485.7	1585.3	331.6	373.9	422.3
YORK COUNTY, PA	1407.0	1476.1	1602.9	90.2	97.7	128.2
BROWARD COUNTY, FL	1398.7	1381.6	1339.6	786.1	873.2	1067.8
NORFOLK COUNTY, MA	1370.5	1379.3	1343.7	120.2	134.5	146.0
CALHOUN COUNTY, MI	1362.6	1520.5	1733.1	78.4	82.5	88.1
DUPAGE COUNTY, IL	1352.1	1458.2	1550.9	351.9	402.3	511.6
SOMERSET COUNTY, NJ	1349.9	1330.7	1479.2	99.8	110.5	134.7
RACINE COUNTY, WI	1348.8	1272.4	1233.0	65.4	73.4	85.5
BRISTOL COUNTY, MA	1345.9	1352.0	1483.1	159.5	170.1	186.8
LEHIGH COUNTY, PA	1345.7	1609.5	1680.8	74.3	81.3	102.0
KALAMAZOO COUNTY, MI	1345.5	1502.9	1765.2	214.6	213.3	214.6
WILL COUNTY, IL	1338.8	1446.2	1680.9	127.8	142.4	171.1
DELAWARE COUNTY, PA	1333.7	1408.7	1526.9	169.6	180.6	197.6
SAN FRANCISCO CITY COUNTY	1329.0	1632.5	1692.4	857.4	893.1	953.1
MONTGOMERY COUNTY, OH	1313.6	1470.1	1534.6	368.0	395.9	430.7
DOUGLAS COUNTY, NE	1305.3	1216.4	1237.1	298.2	325.5	354.0
ORANGE COUNTY, FL	1293.0	1324.6	1334.3	842.7	920.8	998.6
WASHINGTON COUNTY, OR	1253.1	1216.2	1282.3	212.0	213.0	237.6
CABARRUS COUNTY, NC	1253.0	2472.9	3188.9	13.1	14.3	18.1
ONONDAGA COUNTY, NY	1208.5	1313.3	1206.9	407.7	435.1	468.2
SAN BERNARDINO COUNTY, CA	1195.6	1386.2	1593.1	456.0	506.5	674.9
BERKS COUNTY, PA	1191.5	1301.5	1340.6	376.8	377.3	380.2
STANISLAUS COUNTY, CA	1186.2	1287.2	1329.2	117.5	135.3	176.2
DAVIDSON COUNTY, TN	1174.8	1310.7	1293.0	278.0	322.5	370.0
HILLSBOROUGH COUNTY, NH	1174.5	1129.8	1102.8	159.4	172.3	180.1
GREENVILLE COUNTY, SC	1123.6	1312.7	1643.3	121.3	131.0	149.2
JOHNSON COUNTY, IA	1107.8	926.9	879.8	35.9	39.5	43.4
RIVERSIDE COUNTY, CA	1100.5	1133.6	1194.4	495.7	569.6	732.9
ELKHART COUNTY, IN	1090.7	1080.1	1094.1	53.4	58.7	72.9
HAMPDEN COUNTY, MA	1086.2	1099.6	1172.0	97.6	114.2	128.6
BUCKS COUNTY, PA	1084.8	1113.0	1153.5	129.1	142.0	172.5
MECKLENBURG COUNTY, NC	1070.9	1310.3	1352.5	236.3	287.4	407.0
RAMSEY COUNTY, MN	1065.0	1031.6	1022.5	844.1	896.0	951.7

APPENDIX Table 3

The Estimates of Private and Public Capital stocks for Counties by States

(unit: Millions of 1992 dollars)

COUNTY NAMES	PRIVATE CAPITAL STOCK	PRIVATE CAPITAL STOCK	PRIVATE CAPITAL STOCK	PUBLIC CAPITAL STOCK	PUBLIC CAPITAL STOCK	PUBLIC CAPITAL STOCK
	1982	1987	1992	1982	1987	1992
ALABAMA						
JEFFERSON COUNTY	975.6	1015.7	1054.3	280.2	314.5	362.1
MOBILE COUNTY	859.9	953.6	1341.2	81.1	89.7	135.1
MADISON COUNTY	426.2	470.9	540.0	96.8	110.7	139.9
MONTGOMERY COUNTY	357.7	359.1	407.6	67.4	70.3	76.7
LEE COUNTY	299.9	308.7	320.8	27.6	30.4	56.8
CALHOUN COUNTY	290.5	290.3	287.1	42.5	47.0	52.2
HOUSTON COUNTY	266.8	272.7	265.0	67.9	71.4	79.1
BALDWIN COUNTY	216.6	261.6	294.8	49.8	55.3	62.8
MARION COUNTY	183.8	173.6	161.3	7.6	7.4	7.2
ESCAMBIA COUNTY	171.6	195.5	198.7	8.0	8.8	10.3
TUSCALOOSA COUNTY	132.6	154.8	193.9	53.4	58.8	70.5
RUSSELL COUNTY	132.3	134.6	170.0	10.7	11.5	13.9
MARSHALL COUNTY	107.8	132.0	177.4	23.5	25.2	27.8
JACKSON COUNTY	103.8	119.4	207.9	4.2	5.8	9.4
DEKALB COUNTY	84.6	98.0	119.1	5.3	6.1	7.7
WALKER COUNTY	80.3	67.2	59.7	16.7	17.8	19.0
TALLADEGA COUNTY	66.0	100.7	146.4	28.0	31.0	32.4
SHELBY COUNTY	65.3	72.3	89.2	8.4	12.0	19.3
BARBOUR COUNTY	55.2	72.7	71.5	11.9	12.6	13.8
WINSTON COUNTY	50.1	51.5	55.4	4.1	4.2	4.7
CULLMAN COUNTY	50.1	51.5	61.3	19.0	21.6	24.0
BUTLER COUNTY	48.3	48.3	43.5	4.7	5.2	5.8
ST.CLAIR COUNTY	47.2	58.5	60.5	5.5	6.1	7.0
DALLAS COUNTY	43.6	82.1	81.2	38.8	39.1	39.1
BLOUNT COUNTY	37.3	30.1	28.7	4.8	5.0	5.9
PIKE COUNTY	32.8	30.2	27.7	8.4	8.8	11.1
LAMAR COUNTY	30.6	35.6	46.4	2.5	2.8	2.9
FAYETTE COUNTY	25.7	35.9	36.5	2.6	3.1	4.5
CLARKE COUNTY	23.3	26.0	46.4	8.7	8.9	9.2
CHILTON COUNTY	22.4	19.7	17.7	2.5	2.8	3.5
GENEVA COUNTY	20.6	22.3	22.4	4.8	5.0	5.4
PICKENS COUNTY	18.6	20.4	20.6	7.0	7.3	7.3
COOSA COUNTY	15.7	16.1	17.9	0.6	0.7	0.8
BIBB COUNTY	15.6	14.0	14.0	2.2	2.3	3.6
HENRY COUNTY	13.7	11.6	11.0	4.1	4.1	3.9
SUMTER COUNTY	11.7	11.2	15.3	6.7	6.8	6.8
CLAY COUNTY	9.6	10.2	14.9	1.7	2.5	3.1
DALE COUNTY	9.0	10.8	13.8	9.6	10.2	11.4
CLEBURNE COUNTY	8.3	7.1	6.2	0.8	1.1	1.5
CRENSHAW COUNTY	8.0	9.8	14.7	3.4	3.3	3.4
CHEROKEE COUNTY	7.3	6.4	7.0	2.5	2.5	2.8
CONECUH COUNTY	4.5	7.2	18.8	2.9	3.4	3.4
MACON COUNTY	4.4	3.5	3.1	1.1	1.8	3.3
GREENECOUNTY	3.8	4.3	5.4	13.2	13.3	12.6
BULLOCK COUNTY	3.3	3.9	7.1	2.7	2.7	2.7
HALE COUNTY	3.1	7.2	19.5	2.0	2.3	2.8
PERRY COUNTY	2.6	6.3	11.3	6.2	6.4	6.3

FRANKLIN COUNTY	0.2	0.2	0.3	2.8	3.0	3.4
ALASKA						
KENAI PENINSULA BOROUGH	171.1	138.6	118.1	134.8	154.7	173.2
ANCHORAGE CITY BOROUGH	72.0	76.4	69.1	214.7	277.1	320.2
PRINCE OF WALES AREA	47.8	82.1	95.1	1.9	2.1	2.8
KETCHIKAN GATEWAY BOROUGH	22.0	24.4	29.3	32.7	35.9	38.6
WRANGELL PETERSBURG AREA	12.6	13.5	13.0	5.7	7.2	9.2
VALDEZ CORDOVA AREA	2.2	2.7	3.0	120.8	117.9	110.8
ARIZONA						
MARICOPA COUNTY	4197.6	4811.2	5501.9	1658.2	1877.2	2210.8
PIMA COUNTY	989.0	1463.1	1569.2	483.7	533.6	596.3
COCONINO COUNTY	238.4	235.5	207.6	65.1	76.6	88.7
PINAL COUNTY	89.5	81.4	100.0	49.6	77.2	96.9
YAVAPAI COUNTY	88.1	84.3	86.3	45.7	56.5	75.2
MOHAVE COUNTY	60.3	79.8	94.0	43.6	49.1	62.4
YUMA COUNTY	34.0	35.2	42.7	42.3	49.2	63.6
NAVAJO COUNTY	31.5	41.8	43.9	67.1	74.8	85.7
ARKANSAS						
SEBASTIAN COUNTY	920.0	953.6	967.6	28.7	33.0	38.2
PULASKI COUNTY	475.3	458.4	470.5	221.3	231.1	241.2
MISSISSIPPI COUNTY	468.6	441.1	431.3	16.4	19.3	21.1
BENTON COUNTY	347.5	354.1	389.3	11.7	18.1	26.2
GREENE COUNTY	261.9	226.8	216.3	2.1	2.8	5.1
FAULKNER COUNTY	196.1	200.8	254.1	5.5	7.3	11.1
JEFFERSON COUNTY	171.6	197.4	190.3	20.3	26.2	30.8
WASHINGTON COUNTY	153.6	180.4	222.4	47.7	52.6	57.2
WHITE COUNTY	131.4	125.5	139.0	9.1	11.0	13.7
CRAIGHEAD COUNTY	109.3	109.6	110.7	25.7	26.4	25.9
OUACHITA COUNTY	104.8	120.5	140.2	0.5	1.2	2.8
BOONE COUNTY	103.9	90.6	84.9	4.9	7.4	9.1
WOODRUFF COUNTY	102.2	96.1	81.7	0.4	0.5	0.7
BAXTER COUNTY	93.4	110.7	130.1	4.4	6.1	8.2
UNION COUNTY	70.9	60.9	55.2	10.1	11.4	12.5
HOWARD COUNTY	69.3	89.3	125.4	1.4	1.9	2.2
RANDOLPH COUNTY	68.5	58.8	53.3	2.4	2.4	2.5
CLEBURNE COUNTY	68.4	65.8	68.8	1.9	2.2	2.8
POPE COUNTY	66.5	94.4	123.8	3.5	5.4	7.9
BRADLEY COUNTY	64.6	53.6	52.8	3.1	3.8	4.2
INDEPENDENCE COUNTY	64.0	76.7	103.9	16.5	18.0	19.1
GRANT COUNTY	51.0	44.4	40.6	1.9	2.3	2.6
POINSETT COUNTY	44.9	49.3	49.8	3.7	4.5	5.7
POLK COUNTY	41.8	39.2	38.0	9.5	10.4	10.5
HEMPSTEAD COUNTY	41.5	36.0	33.4	14.9	14.8	15.5
JACKSON COUNTY	37.8	32.2	29.8	2.7	2.7	2.8
HOTSPRING COUNTY	35.5	55.2	66.3	1.7	2.5	3.6
DREW COUNTY	33.1	38.2	37.9	3.1	4.2	6.0
PHILLIPS COUNTY	25.0	25.6	31.3	5.6	5.7	6.6
LOGAN COUNTY	22.4	23.9	24.8	3.5	3.9	4.4
DALLAS COUNTY	19.9	25.0	30.9	0.7	0.9	1.1
LINCOLN COUNTY	17.2	13.8	11.7	0.2	1.4	2.7
CLARK COUNTY	16.8	30.5	43.8	0.6	0.7	1.0
CRITTENDEN COUNTY	14.4	22.7	33.3	17.4	20.7	22.5
JOHNSON COUNTY	13.8	17.4	25.7	12.6	15.6	16.5
IZARD COUNTY	5.8	5.6	5.2	2.1	2.8	3.5
LAFAYETTE COUNTY	5.7	4.9	4.8	5.9	5.7	5.5
PRAIRIE COUNTY	5.4	5.7	7.4	1.5	1.6	1.6
GARLAND COUNTY	3.9	12.2	23.3	15.7	16.8	19.1
STONE COUNTY	3.8	3.5	3.9	0.2	0.3	0.5

MONTGOMERY COUNTY	2.5	2.6	2.9	0.9	0.9	1.1
SEARCY COUNTY	2.1	1.7	1.5	0.1	0.3	0.7
CLEVELAND COUNTY	1.4	2.4	3.2	0.4	1.1	1.6
MONROE COUNTY	1.1	1.1	1.1	0.9	1.5	2.2
CALIFORNIA						
LOS ANGELES COUNTY	23949.6	23877.9	22779.0	3763.1	4177.1	4890.9
SANTA CLARA COUNTY	11459.3	12979.3	14272.0	816.9	956.4	1139.9
ORANGE COUNTY	6517.6	6671.8	6614.6	1050.8	1129.2	1349.6
ALAMEDA COUNTY	4398.1	4493.6	5101.2	715.4	813.6	944.5
SAN DIEGO COUNTY	3344.0	3558.7	3794.0	1002.2	1116.1	1343.8
VENTURA COUNTY	1884.8	1938.8	2072.0	337.5	366.4	412.0
SAN MATEO COUNTY	1807.4	1815.6	1965.2	266.3	294.5	346.7
SAN FRANCISCO CITY CO	1329.0	1632.5	1692.4	857.4	893.1	953.1
SAN BERNARDINO COUNTY	1195.6	1386.2	1593.1	456.0	506.5	674.9
STANISLAUS COUNTY	1186.2	1287.2	1329.2	117.5	135.3	176.2
RIVERSIDE COUNTY	1100.5	1133.6	1194.4	495.7	569.6	732.9
SAN JOAQUIN COUNTY	937.9	998.1	1130.2	156.0	177.5	212.7
SANTA CRUZ COUNTY	836.3	859.8	880.9	61.8	75.3	97.7
SACRAMENTO COUNTY	811.2	847.0	867.5	481.7	528.2	604.4
FRESNO COUNTY	670.8	703.6	768.6	273.4	296.1	343.4
SOLANO COUNTY	574.5	552.2	591.4	162.3	180.0	217.2
SONOMA COUNTY	545.3	544.0	587.3	133.3	153.3	188.3
MONTEREY COUNTY	508.6	489.4	456.5	252.2	267.7	285.6
KERN COUNTY	508.1	535.8	557.6	148.1	172.3	229.2
SANTA BARBARA COUNTY	505.8	516.4	536.7	133.0	149.0	173.5
TULARE COUNTY	473.8	434.7	432.1	118.0	134.3	160.6
PLACER COUNTY	380.4	463.6	559.8	66.5	75.5	104.2
CONTRA COSTA COUNTY	336.0	485.2	569.6	331.0	373.0	461.5
YOLO COUNTY	256.0	288.2	307.2	64.5	66.8	71.4
NAPA COUNTY	245.1	270.6	328.0	29.3	31.7	36.4
MADERA COUNTY	198.5	183.0	169.4	12.1	15.0	19.6
MARIN COUNTY	182.7	180.1	174.7	110.7	120.5	132.1
HUMBOLDT COUNTY	182.2	239.0	267.5	73.8	78.1	81.6
SANLUISOBISPO COUNTY	146.3	134.3	164.2	89.8	97.3	112.5
BUTTE COUNTY	142.7	149.2	165.4	33.3	36.9	49.0
NEVADA COUNTY	111.5	120.2	135.3	25.4	29.2	36.1
SUTTER COUNTY	105.3	92.8	93.1	26.9	28.6	30.2
MENDOCINO COUNTY	79.5	108.2	114.8	20.7	23.1	28.5
MERCED COUNTY	69.8	113.6	136.4	81.5	87.3	98.2
SANBENITO COUNTY	68.8	62.8	57.8	5.0	7.4	11.3
SHASTA COUNTY	64.4	78.3	83.9	95.7	99.7	106.7
KINGS COUNTY	47.2	59.8	80.5	27.5	30.1	37.1
AMADOR COUNTY	44.3	38.7	33.9	11.5	12.0	12.6
TEHAMA COUNTY	33.8	49.0	56.7	12.9	15.1	18.4
SISKIYOU COUNTY	33.8	36.9	37.3	24.0	25.9	28.1
ELDORADO COUNTY	26.9	43.4	55.6	68.0	76.1	85.2
YUBA COUNTY	11.2	17.9	19.8	6.8	8.5	12.3
DELNORTE COUNTY	10.6	13.7	12.8	8.7	8.8	9.2
LAKE COUNTY	7.0	8.1	8.9	16.0	18.9	21.7
PLUMAS COUNTY	3.4	8.4	13.1	18.6	18.4	18.1
INYO COUNTY	3.4	3.0	3.1	6.6	7.1	7.8
LASSEN COUNTY	2.2	4.5	6.7	5.5	6.5	8.0
TRINITY COUNTY	1.3	8.2	13.6	3.1	3.7	4.3
COLORADO						
ARAPAHOE COUNTY	1508.0	1508.5	1721.6	329.9	389.2	459.6
BOULDER COUNTY	771.7	901.1	1003.5	112.3	128.8	156.0
ELPASO COUNTY	668.8	842.5	985.6	222.2	245.3	275.8
DENVER CITY AND COUNTY	630.3	660.1	710.9	279.7	352.4	547.2

LARIMER COUNTY	512.4	506.4	556.5	129.4	144.5	167.1
JEFFERSON COUNTY	463.6	531.7	547.2	210.8	243.0	282.4
ADAMS COUNTY	112.1	162.9	190.5	212.4	228.7	241.0
MONTROSE COUNTY	53.0	44.1	42.1	12.9	14.2	16.0
FREMONT COUNTY	25.8	22.5	19.1	29.5	29.7	29.0
OTERO COUNTY	20.3	17.2	15.0	5.6	6.8	8.0
MONTEZUMA COUNTY	12.9	12.4	11.6	12.2	13.3	14.7
RIOGRANDE COUNTY	12.8	13.9	13.3	6.5	7.1	7.4
EAGLE COUNTY	7.8	7.3	8.1	60.1	61.8	69.2
GARFIELD COUNTY	6.8	6.3	6.3	46.6	48.1	50.5
MOFFAT COUNTY	4.9	4.3	3.8	36.9	37.1	35.8
MESA COUNTY	4.9	31.8	40.1	101.0	102.6	106.9
PITKIN COUNTY	4.5	4.4	4.9	24.0	25.8	32.6
SUMMIT COUNTY	3.5	3.0	2.6	26.7	32.0	37.8
KITCARSON COUNTY	3.2	2.7	2.5	6.5	6.6	6.7
PROWERS COUNTY	2.5	10.8	14.6	12.9	14.1	15.5
GRAND COUNTY	2.4	4.0	4.3	39.4	39.2	38.0
ALAMOSA COUNTY	1.0	1.1	1.5	11.8	11.8	11.7
YUMA COUNTY	0.6	0.7	0.7	9.2	11.6	12.5
CONNECTICUT						
NEW HAVEN COUNTY	2324.4	2424.0	2642.6	183.1	215.9	280.5
HARTFORD COUNTY	2170.4	2387.2	2587.3	305.3	346.7	419.7
FAIRFIELD COUNTY	2070.3	2168.4	2236.1	345.9	392.2	454.9
NEW LONDON COUNTY	1023.8	972.9	968.6	117.2	127.4	152.8
LITCHFIELD COUNTY	716.8	726.9	720.0	52.9	57.1	67.6
MIDDLESEX COUNTY	554.0	514.2	492.8	93.4	95.3	104.4
WINDHAM COUNTY	217.2	217.2	226.4	29.5	32.6	38.6
TOLLAND COUNTY	156.5	158.4	160.3	13.1	15.0	24.1
DELAWARE						
KENT COUNTY	1002.2	863.3	797.6	35.7	36.4	38.0
SUSSEX COUNTY	264.5	255.6	291.3	22.3	25.6	34.3
FLORIDA						
DADE COUNTY	2140.3	2041.3	1904.4	1920.8	2035.6	2164.5
PALM BEACH COUNTY	2034.4	2020.6	1925.3	691.6	768.0	907.2
DUVAL COUNTY	1437.0	1376.1	1430.5	357.9	393.7	448.2
BROWARD COUNTY	1398.7	1381.6	1339.6	786.1	873.2	1067.8
ORANGE COUNTY	1293.0	1324.6	1334.3	842.7	920.8	998.6
PINELLAS COUNTY	909.2	1082.0	1176.0	544.1	607.5	678.8
BREVARD COUNTY	698.1	766.3	785.3	143.1	161.0	201.1
HILLSBOROUGH COUNTY	651.8	737.2	785.0	550.8	634.6	755.9
POLK COUNTY	430.6	502.2	537.0	105.4	127.6	154.9
MANATEE COUNTY	357.8	401.7	429.2	47.7	62.8	77.5
SEMINOLE COUNTY	270.9	245.6	228.7	52.4	65.6	91.7
SARASOTA COUNTY	263.5	260.4	263.9	120.6	153.5	203.7
VOLUSIA COUNTY	258.1	272.5	283.6	182.1	201.1	232.1
MARION COUNTY	185.1	223.6	246.6	44.8	50.8	69.2
LEE COUNTY	136.7	141.4	144.7	170.4	190.0	252.2
OKALOOSA COUNTY	75.9	86.3	94.3	36.0	39.3	47.3
MARTIN COUNTY	68.5	70.7	69.3	46.6	50.1	57.7
PASCO COUNTY	48.8	42.2	37.0	73.4	80.9	106.6
GADSDEN COUNTY	48.2	47.5	48.5	10.9	12.2	13.6
ST. LUCIE COUNTY	41.5	53.2	67.3	59.4	69.4	90.6
LAKE COUNTY	36.0	35.4	35.0	47.2	51.0	64.3
COLLIER COUNTY	33.7	39.0	47.5	97.8	106.2	123.1
INDIAN RIVER COUNTY	21.5	30.9	32.3	69.6	77.6	85.3
OSCEOLA COUNTY	17.9	23.1	28.2	21.4	28.6	44.5
HIGHLANDS COUNTY	16.8	16.9	18.6	14.1	16.5	21.5
UNION COUNTY	11.8	12.9	13.1	2.7	2.8	3.3

COLUMBIA COUNTY	11.3	11.8	11.7	16.8	19.3	22.9
CITRUS COUNTY	11.0	13.3	16.3	29.0	32.3	38.9
FLAGLER COUNTY	10.8	17.1	22.8	24.7	27.1	28.8
CLAY COUNTY	10.6	17.8	27.7	22.6	25.7	36.1
MONROE COUNTY	9.7	9.1	8.8	36.5	41.0	46.8
WASHINGTON COUNTY	9.5	11.1	17.9	8.0	8.2	8.5
JACKSON COUNTY	7.6	10.0	11.3	13.7	15.2	17.8
HOLMES COUNTY	6.7	7.1	6.9	6.0	6.9	8.4
CHARLOTTE COUNTY	5.0	4.9	5.0	21.4	26.0	34.0
JEFFERSON COUNTY	2.2	2.1	2.1	6.2	6.3	6.7
CALHOUN COUNTY	2.0	3.1	3.8	1.9	2.0	2.3
DIXIE COUNTY	1.4	1.9	2.4	1.8	2.0	2.7
LIBERTY COUNTY	1.4	1.8	1.9	5.6	5.5	5.2
FRANKLIN COUNTY	0.8	0.7	0.6	3.6	3.7	3.9
OKEECHOBEE COUNTY	0.8	1.2	1.3	6.6	8.9	10.8
GEORGIA						
BIBB COUNTY	2550.8	2376.2	2394.7	98.8	104.5	121.7
FULTON COUNTY	2446.7	2695.3	2539.6	628.8	686.0	761.7
RICHMOND COUNTY	837.9	1113.3	1162.3	110.3	116.9	130.1
DE KALB COUNTY	736.8	849.7	845.3	115.5	135.5	181.7
WHITFIELD COUNTY	546.3	701.9	752.2	50.0	54.3	58.7
NEWTON COUNTY	400.9	349.2	373.5	17.7	19.1	23.3
GWINNETT COUNTY	396.6	698.4	1212.3	82.1	103.4	159.2
HALL COUNTY	306.1	343.9	345.5	43.7	51.2	56.9
COBB COUNTY	289.1	560.1	929.0	79.4	104.5	147.9
FLOYD COUNTY	285.4	287.1	316.4	38.3	44.8	60.4
CLARKE COUNTY	282.4	279.9	281.4	35.9	42.6	52.0
CLAYTON COUNTY	263.3	251.0	256.2	28.6	37.3	47.2
HART COUNTY	195.9	195.3	173.7	2.8	3.0	3.2
BARTOW COUNTY	181.4	165.1	201.2	9.3	11.1	18.9
MERIWETHER COUNTY	176.8	148.3	123.9	3.8	4.4	5.6
POLK COUNTY	170.8	152.1	129.1	20.3	21.0	21.5
LOWNDES COUNTY	146.1	180.9	214.3	16.9	21.1	30.4
THOMAS COUNTY	137.9	139.7	146.4	12.7	14.4	17.3
HOUSTON COUNTY	127.4	113.4	112.8	22.2	26.1	32.0
HENRY COUNTY	124.5	114.2	132.5	23.9	26.6	31.7
GORDON COUNTY	117.8	131.9	132.4	4.2	5.6	9.7
WARE COUNTY	106.8	99.4	97.9	20.6	22.0	23.7
ROCKDALE COUNTY	102.8	111.5	119.8	10.1	12.8	18.8
DECATUR COUNTY	100.2	98.6	97.0	6.5	7.4	8.5
GLYNN COUNTY	98.6	148.5	188.3	19.5	23.9	30.0
LAURENS COUNTY	94.7	99.1	142.2	9.0	9.7	11.0
WALKER COUNTY	74.3	111.6	143.9	10.6	12.5	15.3
TROUP COUNTY	73.8	92.9	129.8	28.8	32.4	34.9
MURRAY COUNTY	69.8	75.0	73.5	3.3	3.8	5.0
HABERSHAM COUNTY	69.5	68.1	85.2	2.7	3.4	6.1
COFFEE COUNTY	60.1	55.3	56.6	27.5	27.8	28.1
STEPHENS COUNTY	56.7	71.1	101.2	0.9	1.7	3.3
SUMTER COUNTY	54.1	63.4	64.7	41.4	42.8	43.5
ELBERT COUNTY	50.8	51.0	55.3	5.3	5.7	6.2
UPSON COUNTY	48.0	63.8	79.7	19.1	20.0	19.5
TIFT COUNTY	46.9	51.4	52.9	17.2	20.7	22.1
EMANUEL COUNTY	45.0	48.6	47.2	10.9	12.2	13.9
BARROW COUNTY	42.1	43.4	57.2	3.1	4.2	7.1
HARALSON COUNTY	41.8	39.9	38.0	4.8	5.3	5.8
CRISP COUNTY	41.2	39.1	36.9	3.6	4.3	5.1
WILKES COUNTY	41.1	39.0	34.7	2.6	2.8	3.5
BULLOCH COUNTY	40.9	48.0	57.6	20.3	21.6	22.8

GRADY COUNTY	39.7	41.2	35.3	5.2	5.8	6.4
FORSYTH COUNTY	37.5	43.7	56.4	17.9	18.7	20.5
MORGAN COUNTY	36.7	40.9	55.3	1.7	2.0	2.6
JACKSON COUNTY	36.7	37.3	38.4	3.2	4.1	5.9
COWETA COUNTY	35.9	47.1	57.0	9.5	11.7	15.0
WALTON COUNTY	34.7	39.7	48.8	6.9	8.5	12.3
COLQUITT COUNTY	32.7	33.2	35.1	10.0	12.4	13.5
GILMER COUNTY	32.5	29.4	26.8	0.7	0.9	1.6
FRANKLIN COUNTY	32.3	36.3	32.6	2.6	3.0	4.2
EVANS COUNTY	31.2	41.5	43.0	4.0	4.1	4.2
CHEROKEE COUNTY	31.1	35.0	50.1	20.3	21.8	25.7
SCREVEN COUNTY	25.6	22.6	23.4	8.9	9.3	9.6
CARROLL COUNTY	23.7	24.6	30.9	12.8	15.6	20.8
TAYLOR COUNTY	16.5	13.7	11.5	0.8	0.8	1.2
COOK COUNTY	15.3	16.7	19.6	1.7	2.0	2.4
TOOMBS COUNTY	15.1	13.1	11.8	5.4	6.6	8.7
DODGE COUNTY	13.9	12.6	13.0	5.3	5.5	5.9
WHITE COUNTY	12.7	17.3	21.5	2.1	2.5	2.7
JOHNSON COUNTY	12.2	11.8	10.9	0.7	0.7	1.3
MITCHELL COUNTY	10.1	9.9	9.1	7.5	8.1	8.4
PICKENS COUNTY	9.8	10.0	9.3	2.3	2.7	3.0
UNION COUNTY	8.1	6.6	5.7	3.6	3.9	5.4
WILCOX COUNTY	7.6	12.5	13.3	1.7	1.7	1.7
APPLING COUNTY	7.4	8.8	10.6	6.9	7.5	8.1
RANDOLPH COUNTY	7.1	6.6	6.4	3.9	4.2	4.9
ATKINSON COUNTY	7.0	8.0	7.7	1.3	1.4	1.6
TURNER COUNTY	6.6	5.8	4.8	9.1	9.6	9.5
PIERCE COUNTY	5.9	8.0	9.8	9.4	9.4	9.2
LINCOLN COUNTY	5.8	5.1	5.1	0.7	1.0	1.9
CLINCH COUNTY	5.3	6.1	7.1	1.0	1.1	1.4
BURKE COUNTY	3.0	2.4	2.1	2.8	4.4	7.4
STEWART COUNTY	2.8	3.7	3.5	8.4	8.1	7.8
WHEELER COUNTY	2.1	2.2	2.8	0.5	0.6	0.7
OGLETHORPE COUNTY	1.3	1.3	1.6	1.8	2.0	2.3
MONROE COUNTY	1.0	1.8	2.1	7.5	8.0	10.3
CHARLTON COUNTY	0.4	1.8	3.9	11.4	11.6	11.4
HAWAII						
HONOLULU CITY AND COUNTY	529.6	537.1	534.0	276.3	308.6	371.4
HAWAII COUNTY	56.8	61.3	61.4	27.4	29.2	39.8
KAUAI COUNTY	6.1	11.0	13.7	16.3	20.2	24.2
IDAHO						
BANNOCK COUNTY	173.2	167.5	202.9	21.5	22.4	25.9
CANYON COUNTY	168.5	175.2	232.4	38.0	40.8	47.6
BINGHAM COUNTY	148.3	148.5	171.2	8.2	9.5	11.2
ADA COUNTY	105.8	121.8	191.2	74.9	83.1	101.7
TWINFALLS COUNTY	73.3	75.0	81.9	37.0	37.5	39.2
KOOTENAI COUNTY	56.5	76.3	94.8	15.6	18.4	28.1
BONNER COUNTY	28.1	36.1	36.4	3.0	3.3	5.5
MADISON COUNTY	22.7	21.3	21.3	20.7	19.9	19.0
LATAH COUNTY	19.1	17.0	18.1	17.5	17.2	16.8
MINIDOKA COUNTY	11.7	24.0	53.5	6.0	6.5	7.4
BENEWAH COUNTY	9.2	9.9	11.5	1.7	1.8	2.0
BLAINE COUNTY	7.1	6.6	6.2	7.1	7.5	9.6
CLEARWATER COUNTY	6.2	7.6	9.2	4.8	4.7	4.7
SHOSHONE COUNTY	4.6	5.0	5.9	13.0	13.1	12.8
FREMONT COUNTY	2.6	4.1	3.8	1.9	2.1	2.1
LEMHI COUNTY	0.7	1.5	2.0	0.8	0.8	0.9
PAYETTE COUNTY	0.6	0.5	0.6	3.2	3.5	5.0

BOUNDARY COUNTY	0.5	7.2	14.7	1.3	1.4	1.5
ILLINOIS						
COOK COUNTY	16483.5	15877.1	15742.5	3500.6	3837.1	4299.7
DUPAGE COUNTY	1352.1	1458.2	1550.9	351.9	402.3	511.6
WILL COUNTY	1338.8	1446.2	1680.9	127.8	142.4	171.1
CHAMPAIGN COUNTY	878.0	826.4	872.4	92.2	99.1	103.6
LAKE COUNTY	666.6	773.1	963.1	192.3	226.3	287.4
KANKAKEE COUNTY	568.7	531.4	504.2	27.4	35.4	42.0
MCHENRY COUNTY	495.2	546.7	616.8	38.0	42.3	55.7
VERMILION COUNTY	409.4	403.2	391.9	51.7	53.9	55.8
MORGAN COUNTY	365.2	382.9	377.8	15.2	15.6	15.7
MACON COUNTY	357.0	451.5	549.2	74.8	79.8	82.3
COLES COUNTY	343.5	362.6	383.2	28.4	31.1	31.7
LOGAN COUNTY	242.9	209.8	196.0	11.4	12.0	12.6
LEE COUNTY	197.8	191.0	179.0	7.5	8.3	9.5
LASALLE COUNTY	196.9	218.9	242.4	36.2	39.1	45.7
WHITESIDE COUNTY	138.2	186.7	195.8	25.5	28.3	31.0
DE KALB COUNTY	131.9	149.3	159.8	31.0	33.3	35.4
MARION COUNTY	129.8	138.0	140.4	17.1	18.0	19.0
EFFINGHAM COUNTY	122.3	159.9	193.9	18.5	19.0	18.9
KNOX COUNTY	90.6	76.3	71.4	14.8	16.0	19.2
LIVINGSTON COUNTY	81.6	114.5	126.2	12.6	14.8	15.6
MONTGOMERY COUNTY	60.5	58.6	55.8	10.4	11.5	11.8
ADAMS COUNTY	59.1	52.7	47.7	38.9	39.7	40.4
JACKSON COUNTY	42.0	36.9	33.8	26.1	27.8	28.6
JODAVIESS COUNTY	35.2	34.9	34.7	10.2	11.0	11.1
DOUGLAS COUNTY	29.1	25.5	23.7	5.2	5.8	5.9
BOND COUNTY	28.8	23.5	19.7	1.7	2.0	2.2
JASPER COUNTY	19.4	16.2	15.0	3.1	3.2	3.3
RANDOLPH COUNTY	17.4	19.7	20.3	7.4	8.2	8.7
MASON COUNTY	8.5	7.0	6.0	5.3	6.1	6.5
MACOUPIN COUNTY	6.9	7.1	6.8	20.9	21.3	21.1
CUMBERLAND COUNTY	6.3	5.8	5.1	1.2	1.9	2.6
WHITE COUNTY	4.3	4.2	6.5	2.0	2.6	3.4
MERCER COUNTY	2.2	2.4	3.5	5.7	6.2	6.7
INDIANA						
MARION COUNTY	3284.0	3380.8	3924.0	478.8	525.1	592.3
ELKHART COUNTY	1090.7	1080.1	1094.1	53.4	58.7	72.9
ALLEN COUNTY	980.0	975.8	990.2	132.7	139.2	145.2
KOSCIUSKO COUNTY	863.6	815.2	906.7	24.3	25.8	33.1
CLARK COUNTY	700.9	592.5	555.3	16.9	22.2	27.1
ST. JOSEPH COUNTY	500.1	520.2	570.3	70.5	74.9	90.3
LAPORTE COUNTY	438.0	392.5	365.3	22.0	25.4	31.9
TIPPECANOE COUNTY	417.3	503.6	579.8	43.7	47.1	54.2
DELAWARE COUNTY	256.9	273.2	268.5	21.8	23.0	27.0
MADISON COUNTY	256.3	238.8	223.9	12.8	16.9	25.0
NOBLE COUNTY	228.2	216.8	232.0	21.1	21.7	24.3
DECATUR COUNTY	219.4	200.4	214.4	3.0	3.7	4.6
HAMILTON COUNTY	216.1	220.3	254.3	32.6	38.1	54.2
BARTHOLOMEW COUNTY	207.1	265.4	357.7	58.5	60.7	73.3
MONTGOMERY COUNTY	186.1	187.9	250.2	3.4	4.3	6.9
DUBOIS COUNTY	181.6	180.1	204.2	4.8	5.8	8.5
MARSHALL COUNTY	179.9	189.7	236.3	12.4	13.9	16.0
WAYNE COUNTY	145.8	168.3	182.8	106.4	104.0	100.3
DE KALB COUNTY	136.6	143.6	170.7	8.4	9.6	11.6
LAGRANGE COUNTY	124.5	122.3	126.5	4.4	5.0	6.2
STEUBEN COUNTY	119.6	138.8	186.4	1.9	3.2	6.0
BLACKFORD COUNTY	116.1	112.5	100.8	1.0	1.3	2.1

WABASH COUNTY	110.7	116.5	129.1	9.7	10.4	11.9
RUSH COUNTY	104.9	87.4	84.0	2.6	2.9	3.6
CLINTON COUNTY	90.5	126.0	199.4	18.7	19.4	19.8
WELLS COUNTY	85.2	79.4	86.6	6.5	7.2	8.5
MIAMI COUNTY	78.0	66.8	63.0	19.8	20.5	22.4
LAWRENCE COUNTY	75.2	94.6	94.9	13.1	14.0	16.1
JEFFERSON COUNTY	74.6	76.4	71.9	3.7	4.4	5.7
RANDOLPH COUNTY	73.8	75.4	70.1	18.7	18.6	18.5
WHITE COUNTY	72.0	71.4	77.5	14.9	16.1	19.1
JAY COUNTY	71.5	66.8	62.9	15.9	15.8	15.7
JOHNSON COUNTY	56.0	61.7	79.7	15.7	18.2	26.1
HENRY COUNTY	54.2	49.0	51.9	15.5	15.9	16.8
MORGAN COUNTY	53.0	72.4	75.6	10.9	12.1	15.3
JENNINGS COUNTY	47.7	47.7	46.3	2.9	3.3	4.0
FOUNTAIN COUNTY	46.8	42.2	42.5	1.7	1.9	2.9
WHITLEY COUNTY	46.0	52.4	60.8	2.5	3.1	4.3
CASS COUNTY	45.2	51.3	64.5	27.0	28.8	31.1
ADAMS COUNTY	43.4	65.9	88.0	4.8	5.6	7.4
PUTNAM COUNTY	43.2	40.8	52.4	13.7	13.6	15.5
WASHINGTON COUNTY	36.6	48.0	53.8	5.2	6.1	8.5
PERRY COUNTY	34.9	30.0	27.0	3.1	3.6	4.7
PULASKI COUNTY	32.6	36.5	43.6	19.0	18.7	18.1
KNOX COUNTY	28.8	30.0	37.8	14.1	14.9	16.3
JASPER COUNTY	23.5	23.3	27.7	8.1	8.7	11.2
SCOTT COUNTY	20.5	31.2	52.4	3.1	4.3	5.4
CARROLL COUNTY	20.3	20.6	24.3	4.4	4.8	5.5
BOONE COUNTY	18.8	19.5	19.4	6.3	7.8	10.6
STARKE COUNTY	14.7	13.0	12.3	4.2	4.4	4.9
ORANGE COUNTY	8.7	9.2	8.7	14.4	14.6	14.7
IOWA						
LINN COUNTY	1820.5	1665.3	1633.9	101.5	110.4	125.0
JOHNSON COUNTY	1107.8	926.9	879.8	35.9	39.5	43.4
MUSCATINE COUNTY	889.7	748.1	751.8	15.8	17.0	19.3
SCOTT COUNTY	431.8	487.4	525.2	98.2	103.2	107.6
CLINTON COUNTY	344.0	399.3	479.1	17.4	18.8	24.6
DES MOINES COUNTY	331.2	294.3	255.6	72.5	72.1	70.7
LEE COUNTY	323.3	315.5	347.2	18.9	19.9	20.4
DUBUQUE COUNTY	322.9	335.5	408.1	51.8	53.7	54.0
HENRY COUNTY	313.5	289.7	277.3	12.8	13.0	13.3
STORY COUNTY	293.3	245.2	214.5	32.1	34.1	38.8
MARSHALL COUNTY	258.6	228.2	221.7	29.9	31.7	33.0
WEBSTER COUNTY	216.1	194.4	198.6	23.9	24.6	26.5
MARION COUNTY	140.4	137.3	134.4	27.2	27.2	28.6
PAGE COUNTY	119.3	112.6	109.4	4.7	5.1	5.3
CERROGORDO COUNTY	100.0	116.8	124.7	21.9	23.7	25.7
JEFFERSON COUNTY	65.7	61.8	71.1	10.3	10.4	10.7
FAYETTE COUNTY	63.4	59.6	55.2	6.6	7.6	9.3
MONTGOMERY COUNTY	56.1	47.0	43.9	2.5	3.6	4.4
POWESHIEK COUNTY	49.0	44.4	48.3	9.1	10.0	11.4
CHICKASAW COUNTY	47.9	42.0	42.6	16.5	16.4	16.1
CARROLL COUNTY	37.0	34.9	55.0	12.2	12.7	13.6
WASHINGTON COUNTY	34.5	30.7	31.9	6.9	7.6	9.2
JONES COUNTY	32.7	30.0	28.2	8.1	8.3	8.6
HOWARD COUNTY	24.3	20.2	20.6	3.9	4.1	4.6
BOONE COUNTY	21.9	19.7	17.6	6.5	7.2	9.7
MAHASKA COUNTY	20.0	20.9	23.4	8.3	9.3	10.4
KOSSUTH COUNTY	19.8	17.4	18.0	9.5	10.0	10.4
UNION COUNTY	17.2	15.7	17.4	5.8	6.4	7.6

DELAWARE COUNTY	14.6	33.1	45.5	12.8	13.3	14.6
O'BRIEN COUNTY	12.9	12.3	11.7	20.7	21.1	21.0
JACKSON COUNTY	12.6	12.6	17.1	14.2	14.6	14.9
WAYNE COUNTY	11.3	11.0	9.3	3.4	3.5	3.5
HUMBOLDT COUNTY	10.0	9.8	9.2	5.7	6.0	6.3
WINNESHIEK COUNTY	9.2	10.8	14.7	4.7	5.6	9.4
CLAYTON COUNTY	9.1	18.0	26.3	12.3	12.7	13.6
HARDIN COUNTY	8.5	11.7	16.9	12.5	13.0	13.7
ALLAMAKEE COUNTY	8.5	7.8	8.6	7.6	9.2	10.3
TAYLOR COUNTY	7.0	6.2	7.4	5.7	5.9	5.9
WARREN COUNTY	6.7	5.8	6.3	12.8	13.9	15.6
SAC COUNTY	4.9	4.3	4.3	7.2	7.4	7.6
CLAY COUNTY	3.9	30.1	38.2	15.6	16.0	16.7
HARRISON COUNTY	3.2	2.9	2.9	6.3	6.4	7.0
LYON COUNTY	3.2	2.7	2.6	4.5	4.8	5.3
CALHOUN COUNTY	2.7	2.7	2.7	14.6	14.4	13.8
HANCOCK COUNTY	1.0	3.0	4.4	6.2	6.7	7.5
POCAHONTAS COUNTY	0.7	1.5	2.1	8.0	8.3	8.4
KANSAS						
WYANDOTTE COUNTY	343.6	450.6	675.1	109.2	122.8	128.5
SALINE COUNTY	304.4	299.0	282.6	17.7	19.9	23.5
RENO COUNTY	108.8	112.9	118.1	46.8	48.7	49.9
COWLEY COUNTY	106.1	128.3	132.9	34.4	36.9	37.1
ATCHISON COUNTY	104.0	88.4	79.5	5.3	5.6	5.9
LABETTE COUNTY	103.7	82.9	67.3	16.4	16.5	16.4
MONTGOMERY COUNTY	96.0	257.7	278.7	30.8	31.4	31.5
ALLEN COUNTY	68.1	61.2	55.9	5.8	6.4	7.3
FRANKLIN COUNTY	58.4	50.6	47.1	7.9	9.1	9.8
CHEROKEE COUNTY	37.3	36.4	33.5	7.4	8.0	8.6
NEMAHA COUNTY	31.3	38.5	38.4	4.6	5.1	5.7
SUMNER COUNTY	22.1	22.6	23.0	15.4	16.1	16.4
RICE COUNTY	20.3	18.6	17.8	4.7	5.2	5.8
DICKINSON COUNTY	15.5	16.9	18.1	15.6	16.3	17.2
BOURBON COUNTY	13.7	14.6	16.8	7.3	7.5	8.1
GEARY COUNTY	11.2	10.0	9.2	14.8	15.3	15.9
NORTON COUNTY	8.3	6.9	5.8	3.7	4.0	4.5
MITCHELL COUNTY	8.2	8.3	8.2	8.9	9.1	9.3
PRATT COUNTY	6.9	6.0	5.4	8.9	9.0	9.1
CLOUD COUNTY	6.2	5.8	5.2	8.7	9.1	8.9
RUSSELL COUNTY	5.4	4.5	3.8	5.2	5.3	5.6
CLAY COUNTY	4.8	4.0	3.5	4.5	5.3	6.3
KINGMAN COUNTY	4.4	5.7	5.6	5.5	5.8	6.1
LINN COUNTY	2.6	2.3	2.1	3.6	4.0	4.3
ANDERSON COUNTY	1.4	1.2	1.0	4.5	4.7	4.8
PAWNEE COUNTY	0.6	0.6	0.6	3.9	4.1	4.4
KENTUCKY						
JEFFERSON COUNTY	6588.1	6294.4	5829.8	122.8	146.5	199.9
WARREN COUNTY	436.1	380.4	324.1	15.6	18.4	21.3
BOYLE COUNTY	395.3	525.8	693.9	2.9	3.1	3.4
MADISON COUNTY	364.3	349.5	326.2	11.2	12.4	14.4
DAVIESS COUNTY	313.9	370.7	412.4	43.7	48.0	52.1
MCCRACKEN COUNTY	265.6	219.5	191.0	14.3	14.9	17.0
FRANKLIN COUNTY	227.9	226.0	226.9	9.1	10.7	13.9
HARDIN COUNTY	192.0	193.3	200.2	16.8	18.6	21.7
BOONE COUNTY	180.9	227.8	279.9	1.7	3.9	7.7
NELSON COUNTY	175.4	179.8	181.7	6.3	6.9	7.7
BULLITT COUNTY	174.2	163.5	153.6	2.2	2.5	3.2
LOGAN COUNTY	130.9	143.4	155.0	3.2	3.6	4.2

MARSHALL COUNTY	119.3	221.0	258.7	2.3	2.6	3.4
CALLOWAY COUNTY	118.8	144.4	177.3	10.4	10.7	10.8
ROWAN COUNTY	98.6	82.1	68.7	3.3	3.5	3.7
HENDERSON COUNTY	84.8	118.0	135.6	6.2	7.3	8.9
KNOX COUNTY	71.2	60.2	51.7	4.2	4.3	4.4
WHITLEY COUNTY	61.5	48.9	40.3	12.2	13.9	14.0
UNION COUNTY	51.1	43.0	39.0	2.5	2.6	2.8
LAUREL COUNTY	41.9	43.7	47.8	3.2	3.9	5.1
MONROE COUNTY	38.5	33.1	29.7	2.5	2.5	2.5
TODD COUNTY	38.3	33.4	30.9	8.0	7.9	7.7
GRAYSON COUNTY	25.5	28.6	30.7	1.5	1.6	2.1
WEBSTER COUNTY	21.8	20.0	19.3	3.3	3.6	3.9
CLINTON COUNTY	12.3	10.1	8.6	1.1	1.1	1.1
LINCOLN COUNTY	8.2	7.5	7.8	1.3	1.6	2.3
GREEN COUNTY	4.8	4.3	3.6	0.5	0.7	1.0
ADAIR COUNTY	4.1	4.2	4.8	1.0	1.2	1.9
HARLAN COUNTY	2.9	2.5	2.3	10.7	11.2	11.2
PIKE COUNTY	1.8	3.2	4.6	23.8	23.5	23.8
BRECKINRIDGE COUNTY	1.0	0.9	0.7	2.0	2.1	2.4
LOUISIANA						
ORLEANS PARISH	806.4	791.2	730.2	366.2	397.0	428.9
CADDO PARISH	780.4	982.3	1185.1	184.7	201.0	213.6
ST. MARTIN PARISH	469.0	393.3	340.0	25.9	28.0	27.8
RAPIDES PARISH	344.9	320.0	323.4	48.0	49.2	53.3
CALCASIEU PARISH	329.6	644.0	1047.0	114.0	119.4	124.3
ASCENSION PARISH	252.1	529.1	663.6	34.9	36.7	37.8
ST. CHARLES PARISH	239.8	362.0	682.9	30.2	33.5	36.7
JEFFERSON PARISH	231.9	224.3	205.7	296.6	338.5	378.3
ST. MARY PARISH	190.2	196.7	184.9	47.8	49.5	48.8
EAST BATONROUGE PARISH	189.9	250.4	378.6	208.2	215.4	223.7
IBERIA PARISH	154.8	141.3	126.8	66.4	70.1	70.8
LAFAYETTE PARISH	132.1	134.9	122.1	192.9	197.5	196.0
OUACHITA PARISH	119.6	170.4	293.5	21.2	25.3	31.3
VERMILION PARISH	69.7	62.0	56.2	53.4	55.2	53.0
WEBSTER PARISH	69.3	89.1	111.3	16.5	18.5	19.6
BIENVILLE PARISH	44.1	49.5	51.9	9.2	9.3	8.9
TANGIPAHOA PARISH	38.8	42.0	53.5	20.0	24.9	29.7
BOSSIER PARISH	37.6	43.5	40.9	39.7	43.1	46.9
GRANT PARISH	25.8	26.6	23.3	3.4	3.5	4.0
LASALLE PARISH	21.2	21.7	19.7	26.3	25.9	24.2
WINN PARISH	19.1	30.8	38.2	5.8	6.1	6.1
LINCOLN PARISH	18.5	19.4	39.3	9.9	12.8	13.9
UNION PARISH	7.1	10.1	13.9	1.9	2.0	2.2
SABINE PARISH	6.0	21.7	31.5	11.4	11.6	11.7
FRANKLIN PARISH	5.1	4.4	5.1	4.9	4.8	4.6
CLAIBORNE PARISH	3.7	6.2	7.9	10.8	11.0	10.7
VERNON PARISH	3.5	3.8	3.7	4.1	4.6	4.9
EAST CARROLL PARISH	2.1	2.0	1.9	2.2	2.1	2.2
CALDWELL PARISH	2.1	1.9	1.8	1.1	1.2	1.2
MAINE						
CUMBERLAND COUNTY	365.8	432.1	417.9	106.1	119.4	139.3
ANDROSCOGGIN COUNTY	297.7	288.7	255.6	30.5	33.7	40.2
PENOBSCOT COUNTY	198.7	268.7	287.7	30.4	36.8	49.0
YORK COUNTY	194.3	217.4	211.6	56.8	68.0	82.0
KENNEBEC COUNTY	118.4	119.1	102.6	60.6	64.8	72.1
AROOSTOOK COUNTY	112.1	121.9	134.0	43.1	46.2	48.6
KNOX COUNTY	57.6	59.9	70.2	18.2	18.7	19.9
SOMERSET COUNTY	57.5	99.5	114.7	18.3	21.4	23.2

PISCATAQUIS COUNTY	24.6	26.9	25.1	3.3	4.5	5.6
WASHINGTON COUNTY	2.1	3.8	6.5	9.9	11.7	13.6
MARYLAND						
BALTIMORE CITY AREA	2499.7	2324.3	2266.8	1400.7	1453.8	1481.7
BALTIMORE COUNTY	1471.2	1615.6	1486.0	365.1	391.8	432.1
ANNE ARUNDEL COUNTY	476.7	640.3	910.5	163.2	189.8	216.7
MONTGOMERY COUNTY	421.0	486.6	453.5	303.6	357.6	409.2
FREDERICK COUNTY	296.6	315.0	327.2	75.0	83.8	98.0
WASHINGTON COUNTY	235.3	255.1	351.6	98.7	100.9	104.8
PRINCE GEORGE'S COUNTY	195.2	237.9	372.0	527.1	576.0	631.9
TALBOT COUNTY	144.7	148.1	157.1	9.7	10.0	11.5
HARFORD COUNTY	130.8	123.7	110.1	84.2	87.5	92.4
HOWARD COUNTY	100.4	93.3	92.4	88.0	100.6	123.4
WICOMICO COUNTY	99.8	102.4	119.5	26.9	30.7	35.1
CECIL COUNTY	59.8	64.3	64.4	20.2	22.1	25.2
DORCHESTER COUNTY	36.8	38.7	37.2	9.3	9.8	11.0
CHARLES COUNTY	35.6	35.3	33.8	37.2	42.5	52.7
CAROLINE COUNTY	30.5	32.1	29.6	9.6	9.9	10.4
KENT COUNTY	23.4	25.3	25.5	5.5	6.5	8.1
WORCESTER COUNTY	22.9	22.0	19.5	16.7	20.7	26.2
GARRETT COUNTY	19.5	19.5	18.5	10.5	12.2	13.9
CALVERT COUNTY	9.2	13.7	15.9	22.5	22.9	26.6
ST. MARY'S COUNTY	5.3	6.8	12.2	8.6	10.3	14.8
MASSACHUSETTS						
ESSEX COUNTY	4237.1	3894.4	3650.5	273.7	298.2	326.7
MIDDLESEX COUNTY	3815.4	3982.1	3879.5	365.2	411.0	467.8
WORCESTER COUNTY	1936.1	1874.1	1874.5	263.7	291.8	315.5
SUFFOLK COUNTY	1433.6	1402.7	1390.3	210.1	245.3	315.4
NORFOLK COUNTY	1370.5	1379.3	1343.7	120.2	134.5	146.0
BRISTOL COUNTY	1345.9	1352.0	1483.1	159.5	170.1	186.8
HAMPDEN COUNTY	1086.2	1099.6	1172.0	97.6	114.2	128.6
PLYMOUTH COUNTY	463.9	434.8	439.8	116.8	132.0	146.0
BERKSHIRE COUNTY	185.6	195.7	205.0	18.0	21.6	26.2
HAMPSHIRE COUNTY	161.0	153.6	150.8	45.9	49.8	53.2
FRANKLIN COUNTY	119.5	139.6	171.1	18.6	19.9	25.1
DUKES COUNTY	1.8	2.4	2.7	5.3	7.7	10.9
MICHIGAN						
OAKLAND COUNTY	3181.3	4057.2	4232.0	452.6	490.1	562.7
WAYNE COUNTY	2557.2	4800.3	6705.1	1440.9	1526.9	1654.4
KENT COUNTY	2026.6	2354.5	2679.8	133.0	152.8	196.8
CALHOUN COUNTY	1362.6	1520.5	1733.1	78.4	82.5	88.1
KALAMAZOO COUNTY	1345.5	1502.9	1765.2	214.6	213.3	214.6
ST. JOSEPH COUNTY	868.9	727.0	646.3	31.7	34.4	36.3
ALLEGAN COUNTY	846.2	857.6	916.9	23.0	24.5	26.7
OTTAWA COUNTY	791.7	868.8	942.0	207.1	213.2	222.0
WASHTENAW COUNTY	556.9	848.2	1012.8	94.1	104.3	131.1
MUSKEGON COUNTY	417.0	497.3	523.7	27.9	31.7	42.9
JACKSON COUNTY	296.9	310.2	315.1	21.6	23.8	28.3
MACOMB COUNTY	197.8	398.2	507.5	270.9	296.7	338.2
LENAWEE COUNTY	179.1	191.6	206.2	34.7	37.2	39.4
LIVINGSTON COUNTY	178.1	232.9	290.1	46.5	52.3	71.9
GRAND TRAVERSE COUNTY	176.4	178.0	193.0	23.9	27.2	36.5
HILLSDALE COUNTY	174.9	166.9	173.4	10.6	11.0	12.2
VANBUREN COUNTY	173.4	178.4	187.7	19.7	23.3	31.0
BERRIEN COUNTY	171.4	200.5	211.3	43.8	48.1	54.8
ST. CLAIR COUNTY	158.5	179.3	203.6	58.4	60.7	69.3
WEXFORD COUNTY	124.2	117.7	127.5	3.9	4.9	6.4
MONTCALM COUNTY	103.6	123.8	123.1	6.4	7.7	10.4

MANISTEE COUNTY	99.8	108.3	99.0	8.5	9.6	11.0
CHARLEVOIX COUNTY	91.5	91.1	93.2	3.3	3.8	4.8
IONIA COUNTY	89.2	101.5	106.9	11.6	12.6	16.6
SANILAC COUNTY	88.5	93.6	98.2	5.1	5.5	6.6
MASON COUNTY	76.5	77.1	77.2	11.3	12.1	13.2
BRANCH COUNTY	72.7	67.0	66.8	7.0	9.2	11.5
BARRY COUNTY	71.7	65.9	64.8	7.6	8.0	9.5
MENOMINEE COUNTY	65.2	62.5	63.9	14.3	14.6	17.0
ISABELLA COUNTY	64.1	57.5	58.5	21.5	22.8	24.5
ALPENA COUNTY	61.9	68.6	78.5	7.5	8.1	9.2
TUSCOLA COUNTY	54.4	60.2	66.7	18.5	20.0	21.6
CASS COUNTY	47.8	52.0	56.7	11.4	12.2	13.3
IOSCO COUNTY	34.4	31.6	29.9	0.8	1.7	6.4
SHIAWASSEE COUNTY	31.4	45.3	56.5	11.2	12.3	14.2
OTSEGO COUNTY	29.3	31.1	30.4	23.4	22.9	22.0
OCEANA COUNTY	29.3	32.9	34.5	4.6	4.9	5.7
ARENAC COUNTY	23.3	25.0	24.6	1.9	2.5	3.0
OGEMAW COUNTY	19.9	23.0	22.5	11.3	11.1	10.7
MECOSTA COUNTY	15.9	15.0	15.4	12.0	13.9	14.7
EMMET COUNTY	15.8	18.5	22.0	2.6	3.3	5.8
CLARE COUNTY	13.3	12.7	12.0	2.4	3.3	5.5
KALKASKA COUNTY	12.2	19.3	27.6	2.5	2.8	4.8
GLADWIN COUNTY	12.2	12.5	13.0	8.9	9.4	9.9
GOGEBIC COUNTY	12.0	12.4	13.4	7.4	7.6	8.8
HOUGHTON COUNTY	11.5	12.5	13.3	16.6	17.0	19.1
MARQUETTE COUNTY	10.9	10.8	11.1	36.7	38.9	42.7
CHIPPEWA COUNTY	10.7	12.6	12.3	2.7	3.1	5.3
LEELANAU COUNTY	4.0	4.1	4.5	3.8	4.2	5.6
ALCONA COUNTY	3.6	3.4	3.4	1.3	2.1	2.6
MISSAUKEE COUNTY	2.7	2.9	3.4	2.3	2.4	2.6
IRON COUNTY	0.6	0.6	0.7	3.6	4.5	5.6
BARAGA COUNTY	0.5	3.3	6.8	14.4	14.0	13.3
MINNESOTA						
HENNEPIN COUNTY	1708.2	2086.9	2372.4	688.9	756.2	894.7
RAMSEY COUNTY	1065.0	1031.6	1022.5	844.1	896.0	951.7
DAKOTA COUNTY	1025.9	884.7	914.1	211.1	229.6	257.3
BROWN COUNTY	638.9	548.8	490.7	20.9	22.2	24.1
ANOKA COUNTY	482.7	542.8	566.0	157.0	170.9	205.2
MCLEOD COUNTY	326.4	326.2	356.6	25.6	28.3	33.3
CARVER COUNTY	258.8	283.0	361.2	65.1	67.7	71.7
STEARNS COUNTY	225.9	231.8	252.1	70.5	82.1	94.8
WASECA COUNTY	192.6	194.6	217.3	6.9	9.1	12.0
LESUEUR COUNTY	183.5	195.3	186.1	20.9	21.1	21.5
WASHINGTON COUNTY	158.4	185.4	247.1	79.7	88.2	111.9
WINONA COUNTY	155.8	162.3	176.7	19.3	20.7	23.1
RICE COUNTY	144.0	151.2	176.8	22.3	25.5	29.4
GOODHUE COUNTY	119.5	122.0	128.4	41.8	43.8	46.7
STEELE COUNTY	106.2	127.9	142.6	9.7	11.0	13.9
BLUEEARTH COUNTY	81.3	87.2	87.4	62.8	64.8	68.3
CROWWING COUNTY	78.9	72.6	85.6	47.6	49.0	50.3
LYON COUNTY	75.7	65.6	64.2	12.3	13.2	15.4
DOUGLAS COUNTY	60.4	57.4	55.3	18.7	19.7	22.5
MARTIN COUNTY	53.5	50.9	49.2	19.7	21.3	23.1
OTTERTAIL COUNTY	49.9	54.8	57.5	26.8	31.1	35.2
FARIBAULT COUNTY	40.5	36.0	35.0	11.0	11.6	13.6
BELTRAMI COUNTY	34.1	40.0	45.0	55.7	58.0	58.6
NICOLLET COUNTY	33.0	50.0	60.6	17.2	19.7	22.7
KANDIYOHI COUNTY	31.3	38.5	40.7	37.1	39.5	43.0

MILLELACS COUNTY	26.4	33.4	35.6	22.8	23.9	26.0
PENNINGTON COUNTY	21.9	25.0	31.8	12.1	13.2	14.5
BECKER COUNTY	21.5	24.6	26.4	7.6	8.9	11.3
FILLMORE COUNTY	21.1	25.5	28.7	10.6	13.0	15.7
PINE COUNTY	12.4	10.5	8.7	25.8	26.6	27.2
WATONWAN COUNTY	11.8	15.4	18.2	11.0	11.1	11.8
RENVILLE COUNTY	10.7	10.0	11.8	12.3	13.7	15.3
POPE COUNTY	10.5	9.0	8.0	5.4	6.8	8.1
LAKE COUNTY	7.4	19.6	25.3	18.0	18.6	19.2
SIBLEY COUNTY	7.0	6.3	6.8	10.1	10.7	11.4
MORRISON COUNTY	6.8	14.0	19.8	13.6	14.7	17.4
TODD COUNTY	6.3	9.7	12.5	15.2	16.5	18.5
STEVENS COUNTY	5.8	4.8	4.6	7.0	7.4	8.6
CASS COUNTY	3.4	3.1	2.7	10.7	12.2	17.4
AITKIN COUNTY	3.0	3.0	3.2	13.5	13.6	14.2
MARSHALL COUNTY	2.5	2.4	2.3	11.0	12.2	14.7
CLEARWATER COUNTY	2.0	2.3	3.0	3.3	3.8	4.6
MISSISSIPPI						
HARRISON COUNTY	425.6	426.2	451.0	42.0	51.8	62.5
HINDS COUNTY	337.4	292.8	274.8	242.4	249.5	256.4
LEE COUNTY	296.1	308.1	393.0	31.0	32.7	37.2
DESOTO COUNTY	271.6	256.9	278.0	16.1	16.9	17.0
CLAY COUNTY	251.4	219.2	227.0	4.4	4.6	5.3
MONROE COUNTY	198.1	190.6	212.0	5.7	6.6	8.0
ALCORN COUNTY	175.0	224.6	273.9	13.5	14.9	18.4
WASHINGTON COUNTY	168.3	195.6	181.2	33.4	37.0	39.7
LAUDERDALE COUNTY	160.5	152.1	159.9	82.5	82.1	80.7
WARREN COUNTY	130.1	124.6	140.8	9.8	10.1	10.6
RANKIN COUNTY	126.7	118.4	124.3	26.2	29.4	32.1
TISHOMINGO COUNTY	116.3	94.9	83.1	3.0	3.2	4.1
OKTIBBEHA COUNTY	111.3	101.5	87.2	33.4	33.5	32.6
CLARKE COUNTY	108.0	96.2	91.7	8.0	9.2	9.6
ADAMS COUNTY	104.4	102.9	122.1	9.4	9.5	9.9
JONES COUNTY	95.0	89.1	90.4	42.3	42.2	43.8
CHICKASAW COUNTY	87.1	77.8	69.8	8.3	8.8	9.7
TIPPAH COUNTY	75.9	63.6	59.4	1.4	1.6	1.8
PANOLA COUNTY	74.9	77.7	116.4	4.1	4.7	5.3
ITAWAMBA COUNTY	71.6	65.1	56.8	9.4	9.9	10.9
MARSHALL COUNTY	71.6	76.6	72.1	2.8	2.9	3.5
PIKE COUNTY	67.9	79.2	80.7	17.5	18.5	18.5
FORREST COUNTY	62.5	73.9	71.1	14.0	18.9	27.4
PONTOTOC COUNTY	62.5	57.4	54.3	9.4	9.8	10.0
LEFLORE COUNTY	61.6	55.2	58.4	14.1	16.3	17.9
UNION COUNTY	60.4	50.5	49.3	2.6	3.0	3.4
GRENADA COUNTY	53.5	67.2	67.9	14.2	14.0	13.6
NESHOBA COUNTY	52.6	58.3	77.6	25.7	25.1	25.0
SCOTT COUNTY	47.1	46.6	51.8	7.7	8.4	9.0
WAYNE COUNTY	42.7	35.7	32.5	11.1	11.0	10.8
WEBSTER COUNTY	41.4	34.3	31.3	3.8	3.7	3.6
LAFAYETTE COUNTY	39.3	41.8	52.2	9.9	10.4	11.2
LAMAR COUNTY	38.9	35.4	38.3	5.4	5.8	6.0
AMITE COUNTY	38.4	37.8	36.1	10.8	10.8	10.8
LEAKE COUNTY	37.7	45.7	43.1	1.7	1.8	2.3
WINSTON COUNTY	35.7	37.9	35.6	13.6	13.2	12.5
LINCOLN COUNTY	31.9	27.5	22.6	20.7	21.6	22.1
HANCOCK COUNTY	31.5	67.0	73.6	6.2	7.0	8.3
HOLMES COUNTY	29.6	23.5	20.0	18.4	18.5	17.8
GEORGE COUNTY	24.5	20.9	17.2	4.1	4.2	4.4

SUNFLOWER COUNTY	24.4	64.0	70.3	11.8	13.1	15.4
PRENTISS COUNTY	23.4	24.9	30.5	11.8	11.7	13.9
COAHOMA COUNTY	22.1	23.7	29.8	45.2	46.3	45.1
ATTALA COUNTY	21.1	20.1	21.1	2.1	2.6	3.8
COPIAH COUNTY	16.8	20.0	26.3	11.2	12.2	12.5
TALLAHATCHIE COUNTY	16.2	14.3	12.6	4.1	4.4	4.6
MADISON COUNTY	15.4	17.2	16.6	13.5	15.1	17.9
PEARLRIVER COUNTY	14.0	16.8	26.0	14.5	15.1	15.7
STONE COUNTY	13.4	15.6	20.8	18.1	17.9	17.8
MARION COUNTY	12.1	14.7	13.7	11.9	12.3	12.2
CLAIBORNE COUNTY	10.0	9.7	12.1	6.8	7.8	9.2
JASPER COUNTY	9.9	11.7	15.6	9.3	9.5	9.7
KEMPER COUNTY	4.5	3.7	3.0	9.8	9.9	9.7
BENTON COUNTY	2.9	4.1	4.1	0.5	0.5	0.8
JEFFERSON COUNTY	2.5	2.4	2.1	0.6	0.6	0.9
JEFFERSON DAVIS COUNTY	2.5	2.2	2.1	7.9	8.1	7.7
NOXUBEE COUNTY	1.9	3.9	6.7	1.6	1.8	1.9
FRANKLIN COUNTY	1.5	4.8	5.9	2.7	2.8	2.8
CALHOUN COUNTY	1.3	6.0	11.6	2.4	2.6	2.8
MISSOURI						
ST. LOUIS CITY AREA	2713.8	2786.1	2788.1	279.3	322.7	406.1
JACKSON COUNTY	2303.2	2411.6	2618.1	455.9	503.1	602.5
ST. LOUIS COUNTY	2258.3	2534.7	2614.6	267.8	289.5	328.0
CLAY COUNTY	1790.0	1901.8	1899.1	49.9	54.9	63.5
MARION COUNTY	705.2	635.3	654.4	20.2	20.3	20.0
GREENE COUNTY	620.9	564.6	538.1	71.1	80.1	97.2
BUCHANAN COUNTY	425.8	406.6	414.8	43.7	45.4	46.1
BOONE COUNTY	324.5	304.8	310.2	157.1	162.6	164.9
COLE COUNTY	313.2	285.2	253.3	25.2	25.7	28.3
NODAWAY COUNTY	268.0	233.0	210.7	4.5	4.9	5.6
JASPER COUNTY	227.1	229.5	236.2	27.0	30.8	31.9
NEWTON COUNTY	129.7	117.3	119.4	2.8	3.6	4.5
PETTIS COUNTY	116.6	146.8	164.9	7.9	8.5	11.5
SCOTT COUNTY	88.1	89.8	92.5	10.9	11.6	13.5
DUNKLIN COUNTY	81.3	76.2	69.2	8.4	8.6	9.1
PIKE COUNTY	75.9	76.5	76.2	2.7	2.9	3.2
CRAWFORD COUNTY	71.6	83.8	90.7	2.2	2.4	2.6
HOWELL COUNTY	71.3	71.5	72.3	0.0	0.3	1.1
ADAIR COUNTY	69.2	60.4	57.4	17.8	18.6	18.9
LACLEDE COUNTY	51.7	57.8	57.7	4.9	5.6	6.3
ST. FRANCOIS COUNTY	51.7	48.3	47.1	6.0	7.6	9.5
SALINE COUNTY	48.5	63.7	81.2	9.3	10.9	11.6
HENRY COUNTY	48.3	40.0	35.6	14.5	14.9	14.6
BARRY COUNTY	45.5	60.0	74.2	6.0	6.2	7.2
AUDRAIN COUNTY	37.1	42.5	47.4	22.6	23.6	24.8
LINN COUNTY	34.9	31.5	31.9	5.8	6.2	6.5
GASCONADE COUNTY	34.2	32.9	34.4	6.0	6.3	6.5
PHELPS COUNTY	34.0	29.4	28.8	19.4	20.4	20.9
CHRISTIAN COUNTY	33.7	39.8	47.1	10.3	11.3	11.9
PEMISCOT COUNTY	33.3	29.2	24.7	4.2	5.0	5.9
WRIGHT COUNTY	29.8	24.3	21.7	1.4	1.7	2.0
CALLAWAY COUNTY	28.0	23.9	22.9	18.0	18.7	19.0
TEXAS COUNTY	27.0	33.1	34.5	5.1	5.3	5.6
LIVINGSTON COUNTY	20.5	18.1	17.8	9.7	10.0	10.3
RIPLEY COUNTY	19.3	16.1	14.5	3.6	3.6	3.7
POLK COUNTY	16.0	14.2	13.5	3.0	3.2	3.7
CEDAR COUNTY	15.6	13.2	11.5	1.5	1.5	1.7
JOHNSON COUNTY	14.8	25.5	38.0	8.6	10.8	13.2

CHARITON COUNTY	14.3	12.7	11.2	1.5	1.9	2.4
WEBSTER COUNTY	13.7	14.3	16.2	0.9	1.3	2.1
MONTGOMERY COUNTY	13.6	12.1	11.6	1.5	1.5	1.7
CAMDEN COUNTY	13.3	14.4	16.8	3.1	5.3	7.3
PERRY COUNTY	12.7	15.6	25.0	5.4	5.4	6.0
MONITEAU COUNTY	12.3	11.6	11.1	2.0	2.1	2.3
WAYNE COUNTY	11.0	10.8	10.6	2.7	2.8	3.1
LAFAYETTE COUNTY	9.9	10.0	12.2	5.9	6.3	7.3
CARTER COUNTY	8.4	8.0	8.1	2.0	2.1	2.1
MADISON COUNTY	7.5	7.1	7.2	3.0	3.2	3.3
PULASKI COUNTY	6.9	6.4	6.7	3.9	4.8	5.4
GENTRY COUNTY	6.9	5.5	4.7	1.7	1.8	1.8
WARREN COUNTY	6.1	10.7	15.7	2.7	3.2	4.0
OZARK COUNTY	3.4	3.4	4.2	1.9	2.0	2.0
REYNOLDS COUNTY	2.7	3.2	3.9	0.8	0.8	0.9
BATES COUNTY	2.5	2.8	3.6	1.8	1.9	2.1
SHANNON COUNTY	2.5	3.6	5.3	0.5	0.6	0.6
CLINTON COUNTY	1.9	1.9	1.8	15.0	14.7	14.5
BENTON COUNTY	1.5	1.4	1.3	1.6	1.7	1.8
OREGON COUNTY	1.2	1.2	1.4	1.6	1.7	1.7
STONE COUNTY	0.8	0.7	0.7	0.7	0.8	1.2
MORGAN COUNTY	0.4	0.4	0.3	2.5	2.8	3.1
MONTANA						
FLATHEAD COUNTY	45.1	87.7	95.1	9.6	12.9	19.1
GALLATIN COUNTY	32.0	35.4	41.0	19.1	20.3	25.6
CASCADE COUNTY	26.0	27.1	28.3	20.2	21.8	24.9
SILVERBOW COUNTY	7.8	11.6	15.2	5.0	7.0	8.1
MISSOULA COUNTY	6.5	49.3	92.5	33.3	34.0	38.5
RAVALLI COUNTY	6.0	7.9	9.9	6.0	6.1	6.8
CUSTER COUNTY	4.4	4.1	4.0	2.5	2.7	3.3
LINCOLN COUNTY	3.4	15.4	24.3	7.1	7.7	8.3
HILL COUNTY	3.2	3.0	2.5	5.2	5.5	5.8
MINERAL COUNTY	3.1	4.1	4.7	1.5	1.6	1.6
SANDERS COUNTY	2.2	3.4	4.8	5.9	6.0	6.0
NEBRASKA						
DOUGLAS COUNTY	1305.3	1216.4	1237.1	298.2	325.5	354.0
LANCASTER COUNTY	569.6	563.5	656.5	120.8	128.8	146.2
DODGE COUNTY	351.7	281.5	235.6	14.3	15.0	15.3
PLATTE COUNTY	238.5	247.1	256.7	12.7	13.4	14.0
SALINE COUNTY	143.2	127.6	122.5	5.1	5.3	5.7
BUFFALO COUNTY	142.7	126.9	125.0	20.1	21.4	22.2
HAMILTON COUNTY	66.9	58.1	56.4	5.9	6.1	6.3
ADAMS COUNTY	37.8	36.0	37.1	13.0	13.9	16.6
RICHARDSON COUNTY	16.5	14.4	13.0	4.9	4.9	5.0
JEFFERSON COUNTY	16.3	13.6	12.0	5.4	5.4	5.6
SCOTTSBLUFF COUNTY	9.8	13.5	14.8	16.1	17.1	19.3
GAGE COUNTY	7.5	11.1	15.3	8.3	8.6	9.7
SAUNDERS COUNTY	6.1	5.2	5.4	4.3	4.8	5.6
MADISON COUNTY	3.7	3.4	3.6	31.1	32.9	34.4
KIMBALL COUNTY	3.6	3.4	3.5	1.9	2.0	2.2
LINCOLN COUNTY	3.0	3.4	3.4	44.6	44.1	42.7
HALL COUNTY	0.8	12.5	16.7	47.7	47.9	48.2
NEVADA						
CLARK COUNTY	304.1	350.7	365.5	428.0	478.6	627.7
WASHOE COUNTY	160.4	164.5	176.9	201.8	233.6	260.5
CARSON CITY AREA	72.8	84.2	96.8	23.3	26.5	33.3
LYON COUNTY	33.2	31.4	33.1	7.8	8.5	9.4

NEW HUMPSHIRE						
HILLSBOROUGH COUNTY	1174.5	1129.8	1102.8	159.4	172.3	180.1
ROCKINGHAM COUNTY	546.1	511.0	499.3	103.1	114.2	124.1
STRAFFORD COUNTY	336.0	335.6	351.0	16.2	17.7	23.0
SULLIVAN COUNTY	316.8	261.8	221.7	8.9	9.5	11.5
CHESHIRE COUNTY	226.2	213.5	203.5	20.5	24.3	26.2
MERRIMACK COUNTY	184.4	199.7	209.3	101.7	106.7	106.9
GRAFTON COUNTY	178.1	178.7	182.5	18.2	21.3	30.3
BELKNAP COUNTY	66.5	65.0	62.9	15.5	16.3	18.4
COOS COUNTY	54.4	89.1	120.2	3.8	4.9	7.3
CARROLL COUNTY	32.4	30.6	28.2	10.3	12.1	14.7
NEW JERSEY						
MIDDLESEX COUNTY	2751.9	2854.1	2891.5	355.2	373.5	400.5
BERGEN COUNTY	2129.1	2040.3	1960.0	321.0	341.7	368.9
ESSEX COUNTY	1661.3	1903.9	2233.5	331.7	352.1	396.5
UNION COUNTY	1529.4	1529.0	1553.5	170.7	186.6	216.2
MORRIS COUNTY	1466.5	1678.8	2033.2	250.1	263.3	290.7
PASSAIC COUNTY	1464.9	1447.3	1422.8	209.8	216.8	228.0
HUDSON COUNTY	1436.2	1387.5	1226.9	212.8	238.2	261.6
SOMERSET COUNTY	1349.9	1330.7	1479.2	99.8	110.5	134.7
BURLINGTON COUNTY	753.3	781.3	807.9	162.2	171.6	195.3
MONMOUTH COUNTY	622.3	587.3	558.0	157.8	195.6	245.8
SALEM COUNTY	608.6	566.0	565.1	37.1	37.9	40.6
CAMDEN COUNTY	579.7	595.1	668.9	289.7	341.4	398.9
WARREN COUNTY	507.8	487.3	496.1	61.0	64.7	67.6
ATLANTIC COUNTY	384.0	324.7	280.3	156.6	178.5	207.0
CUMBERLAND COUNTY	372.6	435.1	436.7	32.8	37.3	46.7
GLOUCESTER COUNTY	331.4	402.2	513.6	55.4	60.7	75.7
HUNTERDON COUNTY	321.5	302.1	278.6	47.5	53.0	63.9
OCEAN COUNTY	119.9	130.7	124.6	294.5	309.7	335.8
SUSSEX COUNTY	63.8	59.0	54.6	48.0	53.6	62.5
CAPEMAY COUNTY	9.2	13.4	22.4	73.7	89.7	106.2
NEW MEXICO						
SANTAFE COUNTY	49.8	44.9	41.5	36.2	41.4	52.4
CHAVES COUNTY	49.1	48.1	46.2	25.6	31.3	37.0
SANJUAN COUNTY	31.7	25.3	20.2	90.8	96.1	101.7
VALENCIA COUNTY	8.5	10.7	15.9	8.8	10.3	12.9
CIBOLA COUNTY	8.0	6.8	6.3	12.1	12.8	14.2
COLFAX COUNTY	2.3	2.3	2.0	9.4	10.4	11.9
LOS ALAMOS COUNTY	1.5	1.9	2.3	14.6	16.0	17.1
NEW YORK						
MONROE COUNTY	9931.2	9005.8	8204.8	608.4	651.0	709.1
NEW YORK CITY AREA	9263.6	8104.4	7587.9	6191.0	6851.3	8060.3
SUFFOLK COUNTY	3420.5	3383.2	3125.0	536.2	600.7	679.0
NASSAU COUNTY	2899.3	2767.6	2468.2	1358.9	1442.7	1526.1
ROCKLAND COUNTY	2580.2	2284.0	1988.4	100.6	126.4	151.3
ERIE COUNTY	1993.0	2220.0	2424.7	928.0	959.0	974.2
ONONDAGA COUNTY	1208.5	1313.3	1206.9	407.7	435.1	468.2
NIAGARA COUNTY	1051.6	941.2	897.7	189.9	197.9	206.1
ALBANY COUNTY	863.9	884.9	806.9	112.6	121.7	141.6
OSWEGO COUNTY	733.8	687.2	612.9	62.6	71.6	92.5
ONEIDA COUNTY	596.5	562.5	497.4	113.4	128.0	150.1
CHAUTAUQUA COUNTY	463.7	488.6	520.3	64.6	74.7	84.8
WAYNE COUNTY	360.6	345.9	347.0	63.2	66.3	72.8
CATTARAUGUS COUNTY	317.4	279.0	260.3	42.7	47.2	55.9
CHENANGO COUNTY	261.5	241.9	233.6	26.6	28.8	31.8
WESTCHESTER COUNTY	249.9	509.1	593.0	517.3	564.4	652.1
ONTARIO COUNTY	205.4	205.2	190.7	54.9	59.1	67.4

RENSSELAER COUNTY	196.0	177.1	170.9	78.9	85.4	99.8
LIVINGSTON COUNTY	178.6	170.1	147.3	17.6	19.8	23.3
WASHINGTON COUNTY	172.9	157.2	157.7	18.3	21.5	27.3
WYOMING COUNTY	147.9	138.3	126.5	14.3	15.5	20.0
PUTNAM COUNTY	133.9	136.1	128.3	32.4	34.5	37.3
CAYUGA COUNTY	133.5	142.2	145.5	35.5	38.3	44.0
HERKIMER COUNTY	128.0	152.0	181.8	31.2	34.2	36.9
ORLEANS COUNTY	121.4	115.3	126.7	17.9	19.2	20.7
CORTLAND COUNTY	119.8	130.7	160.4	43.9	47.6	51.0
SARATOGA COUNTY	118.9	164.0	202.8	47.1	54.2	69.8
ULSTER COUNTY	118.4	149.3	147.5	70.1	77.1	92.3
JEFFERSON COUNTY	117.1	120.7	112.9	64.1	73.3	90.3
GENESEE COUNTY	104.6	108.2	116.2	22.4	26.1	31.8
FULTON COUNTY	89.9	77.1	64.0	19.8	22.0	25.2
ALLEGANY COUNTY	84.2	86.1	79.4	28.4	31.3	35.7
ST. LAWRENCE COUNTY	75.0	90.5	107.8	69.9	75.7	83.6
STEUBEN COUNTY	62.2	67.9	76.5	56.1	63.9	73.1
WARREN COUNTY	59.3	83.1	128.8	26.7	31.9	38.9
DELAWARE COUNTY	50.3	81.9	108.4	46.2	48.7	52.0
COLUMBIA COUNTY	48.0	45.6	41.0	26.0	27.9	31.4
OTSEGO COUNTY	42.0	50.8	50.6	25.4	27.0	31.9
MADISON COUNTY	29.9	38.5	40.4	61.0	63.9	65.7
CHEMUNG COUNTY	29.1	27.6	28.0	29.9	36.7	46.7
FRANKLIN COUNTY	22.0	22.2	21.3	23.5	24.9	28.0
SULLIVAN COUNTY	21.6	19.6	19.7	38.8	45.4	56.1
GREENE COUNTY	12.4	11.1	11.5	12.8	14.7	19.3
SCHOHARIE COUNTY	7.9	13.9	17.2	9.4	12.0	15.0
NORTH CAROLINA						
FORSYTH COUNTY	7133.7	6725.1	5948.1	77.9	85.2	98.1
WAKE COUNTY	3107.4	3443.1	3734.4	111.6	148.8	226.8
GUILFORD COUNTY	2597.0	2674.6	2763.8	129.7	141.4	165.0
ROCKINGHAM COUNTY	1596.9	1507.6	1486.3	14.5	17.2	21.5
CABARRUS COUNTY	1253.0	2472.9	3188.9	13.1	14.3	18.1
MECKLENBURG COUNTY	1070.9	1310.3	1352.5	236.3	287.4	407.0
PITT COUNTY	960.2	1074.2	1443.3	25.8	27.5	34.2
GASTON COUNTY	687.9	815.6	908.1	49.5	53.1	60.0
CUMBERLAND COUNTY	565.7	610.2	652.6	50.4	54.8	60.4
WILSON COUNTY	562.3	660.9	834.7	31.3	34.1	36.6
CATAWBA COUNTY	534.8	576.1	632.6	30.6	33.0	38.3
LEE COUNTY	365.6	354.1	337.3	17.0	21.3	24.5
IREDELL COUNTY	365.3	365.7	390.1	18.5	19.9	23.3
ROWAN COUNTY	341.6	383.4	446.3	11.4	14.6	21.4
DAVIDSON COUNTY	331.4	371.7	410.1	16.4	18.0	21.2
LENOIR COUNTY	297.4	314.7	362.0	36.4	41.4	43.5
EDGECOMBE COUNTY	272.8	262.0	268.8	12.2	13.7	15.6
HENDERSON COUNTY	271.5	310.5	313.3	30.3	30.4	36.9
MCDOWELL COUNTY	261.8	313.0	321.2	4.7	5.5	7.8
UNION COUNTY	256.4	306.4	325.7	8.3	10.4	17.6
CLEVELAND COUNTY	237.4	422.0	490.0	12.9	14.1	18.6
ALAMANCE COUNTY	231.2	316.8	360.5	49.1	49.5	50.4
JOHNSTON COUNTY	230.3	252.9	268.8	12.1	13.8	20.1
RICHMOND COUNTY	194.8	201.4	200.8	4.7	5.8	7.7
WAYNE COUNTY	193.4	229.3	264.2	23.0	24.8	32.6
NASH COUNTY	179.6	224.1	203.2	44.9	46.5	48.0
BURKE COUNTY	179.5	234.7	242.8	11.6	14.4	22.0
RUTHERFORD COUNTY	178.2	209.3	247.1	7.2	7.9	12.4
SCOTLAND COUNTY	178.1	203.5	235.4	5.5	5.7	6.4
SURRY COUNTY	177.8	218.5	268.7	14.4	15.2	17.2

CALDWELL COUNTY	142.6	155.9	159.2	15.5	19.1	21.7
HOKE COUNTY	133.1	142.4	126.9	2.9	3.0	3.3
GRANVILLE COUNTY	122.6	141.6	191.4	3.9	4.7	9.5
STANLY COUNTY	106.2	159.9	175.5	7.0	8.4	10.6
DURHAM COUNTY	103.6	110.1	126.8	42.1	50.6	72.3
CHATHAM COUNTY	100.2	104.2	121.2	8.3	8.7	10.6
ALEXANDER COUNTY	90.9	89.7	87.1	1.6	1.8	2.3
CHEROKEE COUNTY	82.2	77.3	71.5	2.6	3.1	4.0
LINCOLN COUNTY	69.0	102.7	120.8	3.2	4.5	6.2
ASHE COUNTY	58.8	50.6	44.2	3.3	3.4	3.6
WILKES COUNTY	58.7	61.6	65.2	5.5	6.1	7.5
MONTGOMERY COUNTY	55.4	89.5	102.6	2.7	3.1	3.8
MOORE COUNTY	51.9	54.8	54.9	11.9	14.9	19.8
HALIFAX COUNTY	49.9	57.8	74.9	47.8	48.4	48.0
ANSON COUNTY	43.6	61.0	76.2	34.7	33.2	31.1
PERSON COUNTY	37.1	66.4	88.9	9.5	10.2	11.4
NORTHAMPTON COUNTY	37.1	41.5	46.9	7.5	8.4	9.1
CHOWAN COUNTY	33.3	36.3	40.5	1.5	1.7	2.5
PASQUOTANK COUNTY	32.8	37.1	44.1	4.2	5.3	10.6
MACON COUNTY	31.1	31.5	28.6	1.2	1.5	2.3
WATAUGA COUNTY	28.4	25.0	22.5	7.6	8.9	11.2
BEAUFORT COUNTY	27.0	53.3	72.6	12.9	13.8	15.7
HERTFORD COUNTY	26.4	24.8	21.9	4.7	5.0	6.1
DUPLIN COUNTY	22.7	25.7	29.5	4.9	5.9	8.6
SAMPSON COUNTY	18.5	19.0	18.7	8.5	9.6	13.3
SWAIN COUNTY	11.1	9.0	8.0	4.0	4.3	4.9
MITCHELL COUNTY	10.7	24.6	31.8	2.8	2.9	3.5
ALLEGHANY COUNTY	10.3	13.2	16.9	1.4	1.7	2.3
GREENE COUNTY	8.9	8.0	8.2	1.5	1.7	2.0
DARE COUNTY	4.9	5.5	5.8	18.3	19.8	23.6
PERQUIMANS COUNTY	3.6	5.9	7.9	0.7	1.3	2.2
PENDER COUNTY	3.3	3.4	3.3	6.0	6.4	9.4
POLK COUNTY	1.4	4.5	8.0	2.1	2.2	4.1
GATES COUNTY	0.7	0.7	0.7	0.4	0.5	1.0
PAMLICO COUNTY	0.4	0.6	0.7	0.9	1.1	1.5
WARREN COUNTY	0.1	3.2	7.4	6.9	6.9	8.3
NORTH DAKOTA						
STUTSMAN COUNTY	27.2	28.3	29.4	10.1	10.6	11.4
STARK COUNTY	8.1	8.7	8.7	14.4	14.6	14.6
WILLIAMS COUNTY	5.5	4.8	4.1	18.0	18.5	18.8
OHIO						
HAMILTON COUNTY	7105.2	6948.5	7418.3	500.0	543.2	609.3
CUYAHOGA COUNTY	3275.8	2597.1	2408.8	864.1	933.9	1026.2
FRANKLIN COUNTY	2822.8	2633.1	2617.7	443.9	486.0	588.5
LORAIN COUNTY	1631.8	1538.2	1599.5	58.1	67.4	83.0
MONTGOMERY COUNTY	1313.6	1470.1	1534.6	368.0	395.9	430.7
STARK COUNTY	1013.3	1034.8	1085.5	106.7	111.3	123.7
ALLEN COUNTY	771.1	874.7	916.7	49.3	51.7	53.6
LAKE COUNTY	737.0	765.0	844.6	98.7	106.2	128.2
SANDUSKY COUNTY	640.9	659.8	640.1	16.9	19.4	22.4
BUTLER COUNTY	635.8	754.0	782.7	140.9	142.5	149.2
LUCAS COUNTY	623.7	709.4	920.9	320.1	326.7	334.3
TRUMBULL COUNTY	532.4	619.3	673.1	63.6	70.1	77.1
WAYNE COUNTY	472.2	470.6	512.8	52.6	54.9	60.0
LICKING COUNTY	449.5	430.2	415.1	32.1	38.8	46.1
WOOD COUNTY	406.4	410.9	446.5	72.7	74.9	76.5
ASHTABULA COUNTY	396.1	393.0	383.3	36.4	38.7	41.8
CLARK COUNTY	391.9	488.3	524.2	58.2	60.1	63.0

DARKE COUNTY	386.8	357.7	417.8	12.1	13.0	15.4
MARION COUNTY	371.5	331.4	323.2	20.1	20.8	21.8
HURON COUNTY	322.0	368.2	381.0	21.9	24.1	25.1
HANCOCK COUNTY	318.2	360.0	438.5	23.8	25.6	28.3
MUSKINGUM COUNTY	316.6	290.4	280.8	16.9	18.8	23.7
PORTAGE COUNTY	312.8	343.6	379.7	46.7	48.4	51.3
ERIE COUNTY	310.4	347.2	347.7	44.4	46.0	51.5
DELAWARE COUNTY	310.2	331.1	327.7	12.0	13.7	21.6
CRAWFORD COUNTY	285.8	296.6	290.0	13.4	14.4	14.8
PICKAWAY COUNTY	278.4	314.5	375.4	16.9	17.4	18.5
SUMMIT COUNTY	258.4	492.3	659.4	298.8	320.6	366.4
MEDINA COUNTY	254.3	287.6	324.6	47.9	49.9	56.2
WILLIAMS COUNTY	233.4	249.0	285.9	16.7	19.5	21.7
TUSCARAWAS COUNTY	204.2	192.7	187.7	47.6	47.9	49.0
AUGLAIZE COUNTY	194.1	236.0	312.3	22.5	23.1	24.2
CHAMPAIGN COUNTY	193.1	168.9	161.2	13.4	14.7	15.9
SENECA COUNTY	185.0	200.8	182.5	17.2	17.7	18.5
COSHOCTON COUNTY	173.7	193.2	177.3	29.7	29.5	29.1
GEAUGA COUNTY	169.1	167.3	181.0	26.5	29.8	34.2
ASHLAND COUNTY	158.6	147.7	152.8	6.4	7.1	8.5
FULTON COUNTY	147.6	155.6	210.4	18.0	18.8	19.8
COLUMBIANA COUNTY	146.7	142.2	148.1	19.1	20.3	23.2
MAHONING COUNTY	145.3	175.7	194.7	62.0	64.7	71.6
DEFIANCE COUNTY	136.5	125.6	119.1	13.1	15.1	17.9
CLINTON COUNTY	134.1	123.3	121.8	14.8	14.7	14.8
MERCER COUNTY	122.1	129.6	146.6	7.4	8.6	11.7
HOLMES COUNTY	107.1	135.4	130.5	3.2	3.5	4.2
SHELBY COUNTY	105.8	131.7	192.1	18.4	19.0	20.5
HARDIN COUNTY	102.6	93.6	94.9	7.0	7.7	8.9
JACKSON COUNTY	94.1	104.3	125.5	6.0	6.3	6.6
KNOX COUNTY	92.1	92.7	119.0	21.0	21.8	22.5
MADISON COUNTY	88.4	77.9	76.6	9.6	9.9	11.0
PREBLE COUNTY	85.1	92.2	107.3	11.5	12.0	12.7
HIGHLAND COUNTY	84.5	72.0	65.5	8.9	10.0	10.5
HOCKING COUNTY	79.0	77.2	82.7	4.8	5.4	9.2
PUTNAM COUNTY	72.9	75.3	79.9	12.2	12.9	14.2
FAYETTE COUNTY	72.8	78.7	91.6	11.7	11.5	11.3
PERRY COUNTY	71.9	64.5	61.8	14.6	14.8	14.7
WYANDOT COUNTY	50.4	51.1	51.8	7.7	7.9	8.0
CARROLL COUNTY	48.5	50.6	48.9	7.6	8.0	8.5
ATHENS COUNTY	48.5	45.3	48.1	14.1	15.5	17.6
OTTAWA COUNTY	42.7	63.2	65.5	16.5	17.5	19.8
GUERNSEY COUNTY	41.2	43.8	43.7	7.3	10.0	12.9
PAULDING COUNTY	32.5	36.4	37.5	17.9	17.5	17.2
VANWERT COUNTY	28.9	28.0	30.3	6.2	6.7	8.8
MORROW COUNTY	27.9	28.1	24.6	15.3	15.2	14.8
NOBLE COUNTY	16.8	16.4	14.9	4.1	5.2	7.1
HARRISON COUNTY	9.7	11.8	13.6	2.1	3.0	4.9
OKLAHOMA						
OKLAHOMA COUNTY	2715.9	2841.4	2914.5	499.4	526.9	559.1
TULSA COUNTY	978.5	1072.5	1103.1	388.4	438.0	503.2
CLEVELAND COUNTY	343.1	287.6	246.7	117.5	127.7	132.0
GRADY COUNTY	285.5	239.2	226.9	59.3	58.7	56.2
CUSTER COUNTY	264.6	274.3	269.7	18.9	19.8	20.4
MUSKOGEE COUNTY	190.4	200.0	212.6	25.0	28.3	30.3
CREEK COUNTY	158.3	151.6	176.3	53.7	57.9	61.6
MAYES COUNTY	109.7	103.3	100.5	10.1	11.3	11.7
GARFIELD COUNTY	75.6	75.1	84.0	19.7	21.0	22.4

POTTAWATOMIE COUNTY	74.0	86.9	124.7	42.8	44.5	44.7
WAGONER COUNTY	61.8	63.7	72.9	4.9	5.6	6.5
PAYNE COUNTY	51.6	74.7	87.4	107.4	106.7	101.9
ADAIR COUNTY	45.5	37.9	32.7	87.7	84.5	79.6
PONTOTOC COUNTY	25.2	27.5	24.8	57.3	60.6	60.6
CRAIG COUNTY	21.6	19.1	19.0	5.1	5.3	5.9
PITTSBURG COUNTY	21.5	25.3	30.9	13.0	13.3	13.5
BRYAN COUNTY	19.2	18.7	18.0	8.6	8.8	9.1
CANADIAN COUNTY	15.0	13.4	11.6	31.6	33.8	34.4
KINGFISHER COUNTY	14.9	12.6	11.2	13.7	13.6	13.0
MCCLAIN COUNTY	9.9	8.6	8.5	11.7	12.0	12.5
LOGAN COUNTY	9.6	9.2	9.0	7.6	8.2	8.5
DELAWARE COUNTY	6.7	7.1	7.9	4.1	4.7	5.3
WASHITA COUNTY	6.6	5.5	4.6	5.1	6.2	7.4
MARSHALL COUNTY	4.4	5.6	9.0	3.5	3.5	3.6
BECKHAM COUNTY	4.0	3.7	3.0	25.2	25.4	25.1
JOHNSTON COUNTY	3.9	3.5	4.5	1.3	1.5	1.7
OKFUSKEE COUNTY	3.0	2.5	2.1	5.7	5.9	5.9
CHEROKEE COUNTY	2.3	2.1	2.0	5.6	6.2	7.2
OREGON						
WASHINGTON COUNTY	1253.1	1216.2	1282.3	212.0	213.0	237.6
MULTNOMAH COUNTY	753.2	811.4	1056.7	435.3	471.9	527.2
LANE COUNTY	350.7	404.5	482.6	230.9	242.5	254.3
CLACKAMAS COUNTY	304.5	289.9	288.4	74.4	83.1	106.0
MARION COUNTY	286.3	271.8	275.6	65.2	70.1	79.8
LINN COUNTY	225.9	250.2	345.1	28.6	31.7	37.6
JOSEPHINE COUNTY	94.6	97.6	84.1	14.2	15.0	16.6
UMATILLA COUNTY	79.5	80.1	88.8	45.9	46.0	46.2
DOUGLAS COUNTY	51.9	108.2	181.8	33.2	37.8	43.8
DESCHUTES COUNTY	48.5	62.0	75.1	50.1	51.9	60.7
LINCOLN COUNTY	41.6	47.4	44.2	56.3	57.4	58.8
JACKSON COUNTY	40.1	43.7	49.1	61.0	66.8	72.8
POLK COUNTY	34.7	71.3	71.1	9.0	9.5	11.0
HOODRIVER COUNTY	24.3	21.4	26.5	11.6	13.6	15.0
BAKER COUNTY	21.9	21.1	21.7	8.2	8.7	9.1
TILLAMOOK COUNTY	10.9	13.5	16.5	15.6	15.9	16.0
GRANT COUNTY	5.4	5.8	8.4	14.2	14.1	13.8
UNION COUNTY	5.0	11.6	23.3	10.0	10.4	11.5
CURRY COUNTY	3.4	4.1	6.7	6.4	6.8	8.2
CLATSOP COUNTY	3.2	31.4	48.7	12.2	13.7	15.6
PENNSYLAVANIA						
MONTGOMERY COUNTY	4744.7	4558.3	4748.6	221.2	240.9	260.6
LANCASTER COUNTY	1808.9	1963.5	2142.6	109.1	122.2	156.4
YORK COUNTY	1407.0	1476.1	1602.9	90.2	97.7	128.2
LEHIGH COUNTY	1345.7	1609.5	1680.8	74.3	81.3	102.0
DELAWARE COUNTY	1333.7	1408.7	1526.9	169.6	180.6	197.6
BERKS COUNTY	1191.5	1301.5	1340.6	376.8	377.3	380.2
BUCKS COUNTY	1084.8	1113.0	1153.5	129.1	142.0	172.5
PHILADELPHIA COUNTY	1048.6	1046.2	1175.7	869.5	919.5	1003.5
ERIE COUNTY	964.6	937.2	929.2	72.1	77.6	89.3
LUZERNE COUNTY	944.9	905.0	953.8	139.9	148.4	154.7
BEAVER COUNTY	641.3	578.9	559.8	63.3	66.9	76.3
CUMBERLAND COUNTY	545.0	588.7	594.3	123.4	124.9	130.0
LYCOMING COUNTY	542.3	524.4	507.5	45.1	52.1	59.2
CHESTER COUNTY	508.6	476.7	445.4	66.0	73.4	94.0
NORTHUMBERLAND COUNTY	479.3	446.7	415.5	42.9	42.5	42.7
DAUPHIN COUNTY	475.2	477.1	527.6	229.5	243.4	255.7
LEBANON COUNTY	471.5	436.1	424.5	29.0	32.4	39.6

SCHUYLKILL COUNTY	457.3	441.1	469.4	97.1	97.2	96.9
WESTMORELAND COUNTY	428.6	541.9	698.8	152.5	162.3	177.1
LACKAWANNA COUNTY	411.7	406.3	471.4	43.2	48.3	54.4
NORTHAMPTON COUNTY	360.6	377.7	384.9	82.9	98.4	117.6
BRADFORD COUNTY	358.9	357.5	341.0	8.5	10.8	14.4
BLAIR COUNTY	353.9	350.1	329.0	47.7	49.7	54.3
FRANKLIN COUNTY	327.1	304.8	336.9	126.8	124.5	119.7
WASHINGTON COUNTY	297.6	301.8	311.3	72.3	80.3	90.2
CRAWFORD COUNTY	211.8	236.5	234.7	11.8	14.0	19.2
MERCER COUNTY	211.6	194.2	190.6	32.2	36.1	44.6
BUTLER COUNTY	202.4	306.2	355.9	56.4	58.0	64.7
MCKEAN COUNTY	183.2	225.9	259.7	11.0	14.0	16.2
JEFFERSON COUNTY	161.4	160.7	164.3	14.6	15.0	15.4
CENTRE COUNTY	159.1	170.4	195.0	44.2	47.3	53.5
MIFFLIN COUNTY	138.4	134.4	127.1	28.7	28.8	29.8
FAYETTE COUNTY	136.7	140.7	133.9	23.3	24.8	28.2
ADAMS COUNTY	131.0	150.3	192.2	18.8	21.4	26.1
LAWRENCE COUNTY	119.5	137.5	144.2	43.3	44.4	46.5
ALLEGHENY COUNTY	119.1	333.4	576.2	824.5	868.2	989.9
UNION COUNTY	110.9	135.7	130.8	5.7	6.6	8.5
ELK COUNTY	108.9	125.2	171.8	5.6	6.2	8.3
TIOGA COUNTY	107.3	108.5	103.0	27.5	29.8	32.1
HUNTINGDON COUNTY	102.1	89.9	86.0	18.2	18.6	18.8
CLARION COUNTY	95.6	84.4	76.2	5.1	5.5	7.4
ARMSTRONG COUNTY	92.5	88.3	85.1	44.5	47.4	46.5
SOMERSET COUNTY	79.7	80.3	85.3	17.7	19.5	23.5
CLEARFIELD COUNTY	77.5	74.4	66.0	45.7	46.6	45.7
CARBON COUNTY	68.4	78.8	93.2	11.6	13.1	17.0
INDIANA COUNTY	67.5	59.3	53.0	12.2	15.0	19.3
WAYNE COUNTY	67.5	56.1	47.8	41.0	41.5	45.1
BEDFORD COUNTY	65.6	62.2	59.4	5.6	6.4	8.2
VENANGO COUNTY	52.8	46.1	39.9	41.4	44.3	47.2
SNYDER COUNTY	28.9	32.2	39.4	8.5	9.2	9.7
POTTER COUNTY	14.7	16.2	18.3	1.3	1.5	2.0
PERRY COUNTY	8.3	10.2	11.7	3.2	5.0	11.9
WARREN COUNTY	0.4	76.0	109.0	8.8	15.0	20.0
RHODE ISLAND						
PROVIDENCE COUNTY	1519.7	1470.9	1306.4	221.5	225.4	230.1
KENT COUNTY	434.2	421.9	426.9	22.0	24.6	29.1
WASHINGTON COUNTY	277.1	245.0	248.0	26.8	28.2	31.0
NEWPORT COUNTY	186.5	188.8	161.8	9.9	11.8	13.5
BRISTOL COUNTY	50.9	44.9	43.8	23.6	23.9	24.7
SOUTH CAROLINA						
AIKEN COUNTY	2692.9	2310.9	1965.1	28.6	31.8	36.7
GREENVILLE COUNTY	1123.6	1312.7	1643.3	121.3	131.0	149.2
RICHLAND COUNTY	541.7	796.7	729.4	137.6	150.1	171.8
SPARTANBURG COUNTY	505.7	591.8	911.2	87.0	93.3	102.9
FLORENCE COUNTY	368.9	443.6	442.7	26.5	28.8	35.0
KERSHAW COUNTY	353.8	422.3	376.6	4.0	5.1	9.2
YORK COUNTY	318.6	446.0	471.7	36.9	42.5	61.6
PICKENS COUNTY	277.0	354.0	394.1	5.3	8.2	13.2
OCONEE COUNTY	267.1	328.9	296.6	25.2	25.5	25.2
MARION COUNTY	222.9	204.8	195.5	12.4	12.8	13.6
GREENWOOD COUNTY	200.0	211.7	303.1	42.6	43.7	47.6
DARLINGTON COUNTY	195.8	202.7	188.0	5.1	6.9	9.5
CHARLESTON COUNTY	184.6	251.0	445.0	195.3	205.4	229.3
CHESTERFIELD COUNTY	181.4	196.0	247.6	12.9	13.9	14.6
CHESTER COUNTY	179.8	176.3	198.6	11.5	11.8	12.9

BERKELEY COUNTY	162.1	155.5	156.0	42.5	44.1	46.7
ANDERSON COUNTY	157.4	171.7	238.1	14.6	16.1	23.5
CHEROKEE COUNTY	132.4	198.8	201.0	27.5	27.4	26.7
SUMTER COUNTY	127.6	144.1	197.8	37.1	42.1	45.9
ORANGEBURG COUNTY	123.3	149.2	180.2	81.7	82.6	80.5
WILLIAMSBURG COUNTY	117.9	114.5	146.3	11.5	12.5	13.2
HORRY COUNTY	107.3	126.7	142.7	122.6	133.1	140.0
LAURENS COUNTY	105.0	114.0	129.0	14.2	15.2	17.5
UNION COUNTY	98.1	108.7	114.7	2.0	2.5	3.4
NEWBERRY COUNTY	70.1	100.1	89.4	3.8	4.5	5.4
MARLBORO COUNTY	66.8	66.4	85.7	7.4	7.5	7.4
ALLENDALE COUNTY	48.8	46.2	69.4	0.7	1.9	2.8
FAIRFIELD COUNTY	47.4	63.5	83.7	19.2	21.4	21.5
DORCHESTER COUNTY	40.8	87.7	84.5	5.1	8.2	14.8
HAMPTON COUNTY	38.0	36.0	31.4	3.3	3.9	4.3
EDGEFIELD COUNTY	27.6	24.3	22.1	0.6	0.7	1.2
COLLETON COUNTY	24.1	29.9	40.0	0.8	1.1	2.0
BEAUFORT COUNTY	23.1	24.2	23.9	30.5	34.3	45.0
CLARENDON COUNTY	19.3	18.7	15.7	9.3	9.4	9.3
DILLON COUNTY	17.5	18.7	26.8	1.3	1.6	2.1
BAMBERG COUNTY	16.5	15.6	16.8	5.1	6.0	6.3
JASPER COUNTY	8.5	9.0	8.9	2.5	3.9	5.2
ABBEVILLE COUNTY	7.8	10.9	21.8	1.7	1.9	2.2
LANCASTER COUNTY	4.3	5.6	5.6	13.8	14.0	14.9
SOUTH DAKOTA						
BROWN COUNTY	117.2	104.8	96.1	9.4	11.5	14.3
PENNINGTON COUNTY	75.9	74.1	72.9	36.9	42.0	56.9
CODINGTON COUNTY	53.5	55.0	58.5	20.5	20.4	21.0
LAKE COUNTY	25.2	21.8	20.2	2.4	2.8	3.2
DAVISON COUNTY	22.6	20.2	21.6	10.7	11.8	13.3
YANKTON COUNTY	17.1	24.4	38.0	22.8	22.6	21.9
HUGHES COUNTY	5.4	7.2	9.9	5.1	5.6	6.4
MEADE COUNTY	2.4	3.7	4.3	14.2	15.2	15.2
BRULE COUNTY	1.7	1.6	1.7	4.2	4.2	4.2
LINCOLN COUNTY	0.4	0.4	0.5	7.1	7.4	8.3
TENNESSEE						
DAVIDSON COUNTY	1174.8	1310.7	1293.0	278.0	322.5	370.0
HAMILTON COUNTY	714.2	730.5	831.7	357.1	362.8	368.0
KNOX COUNTY	649.6	613.9	640.5	108.0	114.7	132.5
BRADLEY COUNTY	584.2	632.0	799.8	28.2	32.7	39.3
PUTNAM COUNTY	451.8	406.4	421.7	21.0	21.6	24.2
GREENE COUNTY	291.6	272.3	245.8	13.5	14.7	16.8
WARREN COUNTY	288.0	249.4	241.7	4.2	4.9	7.4
HAWKINS COUNTY	277.8	277.0	297.4	6.1	6.8	7.9
OBION COUNTY	237.1	210.2	173.2	13.5	16.5	18.4
GIBSON COUNTY	206.1	204.9	202.1	17.4	18.2	19.4
MCMINN COUNTY	201.3	237.4	240.7	16.2	16.6	18.3
COFFEE COUNTY	188.4	168.8	189.3	21.9	23.4	24.7
MARSHALL COUNTY	182.3	208.5	236.7	2.7	3.7	5.5
HAMBLEN COUNTY	171.2	198.2	258.5	34.0	33.3	32.5
HARDIN COUNTY	166.8	160.9	186.1	3.1	4.3	5.8
GILES COUNTY	153.7	133.1	125.3	7.1	7.2	7.8
SUMNER COUNTY	149.8	155.2	226.5	39.0	41.5	46.3
LAUDERDALE COUNTY	140.5	123.5	115.4	6.7	8.4	9.3
MCNAIRY COUNTY	124.5	112.9	103.9	9.1	9.8	10.5
COCKE COUNTY	114.6	146.4	170.6	13.0	13.4	13.2
RHEA COUNTY	103.0	89.7	76.5	2.6	3.1	3.7
DYER COUNTY	97.4	98.6	126.9	3.4	4.3	7.6

HENDERSON COUNTY	77.8	77.7	85.4	3.1	4.2	5.5
CLAY COUNTY	68.7	62.1	51.6	2.3	2.4	2.5
BEDFORD COUNTY	68.6	84.7	108.2	2.7	4.1	5.8
WILLIAMSON COUNTY	66.1	67.0	75.4	33.6	38.8	47.8
HICKMAN COUNTY	63.7	52.5	46.7	1.1	1.3	2.5
CUMBERLAND COUNTY	58.1	63.7	74.7	5.9	6.2	7.2
CLAIBORNE COUNTY	54.6	54.9	80.4	2.7	3.0	3.5
JACKSON COUNTY	52.0	48.3	40.2	1.6	1.8	2.0
MACON COUNTY	51.9	49.5	51.7	2.3	2.7	3.2
WAYNE COUNTY	50.9	42.3	45.6	2.2	2.5	2.9
WILSON COUNTY	50.4	55.8	63.8	15.6	19.1	28.4
JEFFERSON COUNTY	44.6	44.3	49.6	3.3	3.8	4.7
HAYWOOD COUNTY	44.0	43.3	39.9	5.8	6.7	7.5
CARROLL COUNTY	41.6	51.5	56.1	16.3	17.1	17.4
HENRY COUNTY	40.2	36.2	35.8	5.6	6.8	8.6
FAYETTE COUNTY	37.6	48.9	75.8	2.7	3.4	4.6
SEVIER COUNTY	34.1	42.4	40.7	19.3	21.8	27.7
WHITE COUNTY	33.9	38.9	43.5	2.9	3.1	3.5
LINCOLN COUNTY	29.0	28.0	31.1	5.5	5.9	8.0
CARTER COUNTY	28.3	35.4	38.7	9.4	10.0	10.8
FRANKLIN COUNTY	23.4	29.5	47.2	9.7	10.1	11.2
MONROE COUNTY	21.9	24.7	63.7	7.6	8.1	8.7
TROUSDALE COUNTY	19.4	17.5	15.8	0.6	0.8	0.9
CAMPBELL COUNTY	18.8	17.1	14.8	7.7	8.3	8.7
SCOTT COUNTY	14.2	16.0	18.3	1.9	2.3	3.7
PERRY COUNTY	13.5	14.2	19.0	0.8	1.2	1.8
OVERTON COUNTY	11.0	11.9	25.9	2.1	3.0	4.0
HARDEMAN COUNTY	8.4	7.7	7.1	3.9	4.8	5.8
DECATUR COUNTY	8.0	10.9	19.7	2.1	2.3	2.6
GRUNDY COUNTY	2.1	2.0	2.0	1.4	1.6	1.9
FENTRESS COUNTY	0.9	14.6	31.7	1.8	2.0	3.4
TEXAS						
DALLAS COUNTY	5598.7	5667.1	5556.8	1170.7	1346.8	1641.3
HARRIS COUNTY	4343.0	5035.8	6126.4	2996.4	3280.7	3530.2
TRAVIS COUNTY	1632.5	2034.7	2787.5	345.3	428.2	519.5
ELPASO COUNTY	1035.6	898.2	877.2	230.8	261.0	319.9
BEXAR COUNTY	945.6	935.4	933.5	540.8	667.0	792.3
MCLENNAN COUNTY	750.2	799.2	795.3	41.3	49.2	61.5
DENTON COUNTY	685.4	753.1	799.0	99.4	118.9	145.8
COLLIN COUNTY	538.9	650.2	766.6	128.1	155.1	196.6
GRAYSON COUNTY	471.0	446.1	416.6	34.9	41.7	49.3
FORTBEND COUNTY	426.7	470.1	502.9	124.8	135.3	154.1
ELLIS COUNTY	399.0	400.4	372.7	21.1	26.5	30.8
BRAZORIA COUNTY	311.6	721.2	1213.0	123.3	129.3	134.7
WILLIAMSON COUNTY	286.6	254.5	240.1	70.9	86.3	107.9
CAMERON COUNTY	265.1	285.3	296.7	98.9	117.8	152.6
HUNT COUNTY	258.8	286.4	312.1	48.2	48.8	48.8
SMITH COUNTY	257.1	256.9	288.3	65.6	70.8	75.6
BROWN COUNTY	250.1	247.5	234.1	13.2	13.9	14.3
LUBBOCK COUNTY	210.7	230.4	247.1	95.3	108.0	132.2
HIDALGO COUNTY	206.8	207.3	244.7	149.3	168.7	197.1
ECTOR COUNTY	181.4	174.4	150.1	113.0	114.9	117.3
GUADALUPE COUNTY	168.3	200.4	275.2	11.4	14.6	18.6
HOPKINS COUNTY	106.1	117.1	106.4	12.1	12.3	12.2
MIDLAND COUNTY	103.9	94.3	79.6	90.9	93.8	99.8
WASHINGTON COUNTY	103.3	95.3	98.6	14.6	16.5	17.4
BRAZOS COUNTY	96.1	97.3	96.4	55.5	62.0	70.5
TOMGREEN COUNTY	91.4	87.5	94.6	25.5	27.9	29.7

CHEROKEE COUNTY	88.4	93.7	100.6	5.9	6.7	7.5
NAVARRO COUNTY	87.4	83.2	78.8	35.0	35.6	35.6
ANGELINA COUNTY	86.5	91.4	94.1	48.4	50.5	50.7
MONTGOMERY COUNTY	79.8	84.9	104.8	115.1	124.1	131.3
NACOGDOCHES COUNTY	74.4	71.0	82.0	44.6	45.7	45.0
TAYLOR COUNTY	73.1	72.4	75.2	31.5	35.8	44.6
POLK COUNTY	69.8	72.1	65.2	5.4	7.3	9.2
JOHNSON COUNTY	68.9	68.5	63.9	33.6	34.6	36.4
ERATH COUNTY	52.9	52.2	53.4	3.8	4.2	4.6
KAUFMAN COUNTY	50.8	45.4	48.8	18.5	23.0	25.7
YOUNG COUNTY	48.8	42.8	35.5	7.3	7.5	7.9
GRIMES COUNTY	46.0	55.9	50.0	3.9	4.5	5.0
LAVACA COUNTY	43.4	37.3	32.5	3.1	3.5	4.1
COOKE COUNTY	42.6	36.2	30.8	11.4	12.2	13.5
COMAL COUNTY	39.8	49.3	52.3	7.8	11.6	15.5
PALOPINTO COUNTY	35.3	31.3	30.3	13.7	15.0	16.8
HAYS COUNTY	35.2	35.0	44.6	36.1	41.7	47.5
REDRIVER COUNTY	29.8	27.7	23.4	3.1	3.4	4.0
BURNET COUNTY	26.9	29.4	29.0	6.6	9.1	11.1
MAVERICK COUNTY	25.4	19.7	16.3	9.6	10.4	12.3
NOLAN COUNTY	25.4	22.4	19.2	12.8	12.8	12.2
MONTAGUE COUNTY	25.2	22.3	20.3	9.8	10.2	11.4
HENDERSON COUNTY	23.4	21.6	19.3	10.5	14.2	17.8
COMANCHE COUNTY	22.7	18.3	14.6	4.0	4.9	5.4
HILL COUNTY	22.2	21.5	18.4	6.1	7.5	8.9
DEWITT COUNTY	20.2	18.5	15.0	16.3	16.6	16.4
COLORADO COUNTY	19.3	16.8	15.2	10.8	11.1	11.3
WHARTON COUNTY	18.7	22.6	51.8	16.5	17.6	18.9
CASS COUNTY	18.6	16.6	16.6	13.7	14.8	16.4
DEAFSMITH COUNTY	18.5	22.6	37.9	3.0	3.8	4.4
RUSK COUNTY	17.4	18.6	22.1	16.7	18.0	18.3
AUSTIN COUNTY	17.3	17.1	14.6	17.8	18.2	17.9
HOCKLEY COUNTY	16.5	17.2	14.2	19.0	19.9	20.4
HOUSTON COUNTY	16.4	16.9	14.7	2.9	3.4	4.1
VANZANDT COUNTY	15.7	14.4	13.0	10.0	11.2	13.3
RUNNELS COUNTY	14.1	18.0	27.2	4.7	4.9	6.2
KERR COUNTY	14.0	13.3	11.9	23.5	25.0	25.1
FANNIN COUNTY	12.6	10.7	9.4	3.3	4.0	5.9
SHELBY COUNTY	12.2	14.8	19.7	4.8	6.4	8.0
ROCKWALL COUNTY	12.1	13.1	19.9	11.2	12.3	15.2
HAMILTON COUNTY	10.0	11.8	10.7	0.8	1.0	1.3
NEWTON COUNTY	8.9	13.8	13.0	6.6	6.9	6.9
FAYETTE COUNTY	8.2	9.1	12.2	6.1	7.0	8.4
LIMESTONE COUNTY	7.8	6.9	8.9	6.0	7.2	7.9
EASTLAND COUNTY	7.4	7.0	5.8	5.3	6.1	6.8
WOOD COUNTY	6.6	5.7	5.0	19.6	21.4	23.0
TYLER COUNTY	5.9	7.8	8.4	9.7	10.3	10.4
SCURRY COUNTY	5.6	5.0	4.2	8.9	9.0	8.9
STEPHENS COUNTY	5.2	4.9	4.9	1.9	2.1	2.2
BASTROP COUNTY	4.8	4.0	4.1	8.1	9.3	10.9
HOOD COUNTY	4.7	3.9	3.8	4.7	6.5	9.1
BURLESON COUNTY	4.0	3.4	3.0	11.4	11.9	11.7
GILLESPIE COUNTY	2.7	3.1	2.8	3.6	3.7	4.0
WISE COUNTY	2.7	11.3	23.6	15.8	16.9	20.2
DAWSON COUNTY	2.6	2.3	2.3	10.8	10.5	10.0
CALDWELL COUNTY	2.4	3.0	3.1	6.0	6.7	7.3
KENDALL COUNTY	2.3	2.1	2.1	4.1	4.7	5.2
ARANSAS COUNTY	2.1	3.1	2.9	13.6	15.0	15.6

WILSON COUNTY	1.9	1.6	1.3	4.5	5.4	6.7
SWISHER COUNTY	1.0	0.9	0.8	2.3	2.9	3.5
MARION COUNTY	0.8	1.0	1.2	1.5	2.7	3.3
SANAUGUSTINE COUNTY	0.7	0.9	1.5	2.8	3.4	3.6
FREESTONE COUNTY	0.6	0.6	0.8	9.1	9.4	9.4
TRINITY COUNTY	0.5	1.0	2.1	3.0	3.8	4.3
UTAH						
SALTLAKE COUNTY	1426.9	1485.7	1585.3	331.6	373.9	422.3
DAVIS COUNTY	272.7	254.8	272.1	95.7	102.0	113.3
WEBER COUNTY	213.5	246.4	351.0	59.0	62.5	67.9
CACHE COUNTY	176.5	178.2	200.5	32.7	34.3	37.6
UTAH COUNTY	50.9	190.9	301.3	101.3	108.1	115.8
IRON COUNTY	18.7	16.6	15.3	26.6	26.4	25.8
TOOELE COUNTY	18.6	22.0	22.8	7.6	8.4	10.3
SEVIER COUNTY	2.6	2.9	3.4	19.5	19.9	19.6
VERMONT						
RUTLAND COUNTY	196.2	190.3	193.4	10.4	12.0	13.7
WINDHAM COUNTY	116.6	111.7	104.7	19.1	20.2	21.2
BENNINGTON COUNTY	96.6	88.5	88.8	3.0	3.7	4.8
WINDSOR COUNTY	83.5	77.2	69.1	17.5	17.9	19.0
WASHINGTON COUNTY	48.3	68.5	71.6	12.5	13.6	14.9
ORANGE COUNTY	27.9	32.8	30.5	2.8	3.3	3.9
FRANKLIN COUNTY	24.3	33.1	42.9	9.9	12.2	13.6
VIRGINIA						
RICHMOND CITY AREA	7939.1	7911.2	7469.7	106.1	121.5	142.3
NORFOLK CITY AREA	871.1	876.5	750.9	124.7	149.3	185.2
LYNCHBURG CITY AREA	666.2	640.1	645.0	40.9	42.1	45.4
ROCKINGHAM COUNTY	627.7	652.7	551.4	4.8	6.3	8.5
HENRICO COUNTY	553.0	521.6	507.2	69.6	84.3	105.7
ROANOKE CITY AREA	497.8	542.2	541.4	54.3	59.1	67.4
CAMPBELL COUNTY	414.8	381.5	368.0	7.4	7.9	9.0
AUGUSTA COUNTY	311.7	341.9	313.2	4.0	4.1	5.3
DANVILLE CITY AREA	307.6	303.4	302.9	7.7	8.9	11.6
SUFFOLK CITY AREA	274.7	225.8	190.5	4.8	6.2	7.8
HENRY COUNTY	249.3	271.8	263.7	4.9	6.9	11.9
MONTGOMERY COUNTY	220.2	219.7	218.7	9.9	11.0	14.2
FAIRFAX COUNTY	195.9	249.1	296.6	262.0	312.1	370.9
CHESTERFIELD COUNTY	189.0	219.7	254.4	153.1	167.8	182.1
WINCHESTER CITY AREA	170.7	241.1	256.2	13.8	15.1	16.6
CHARLOTTESVILLE CITY	154.5	195.9	232.4	5.3	5.9	8.9
MECKLENBURG COUNTY	136.6	124.0	125.0	3.5	3.8	4.7
HOPEWELL CITY AREA	124.0	218.1	204.1	9.6	9.7	10.3
RADFORD CITY AREA	118.3	97.9	84.2	3.8	4.1	4.1
BRISTOL CITY AREA	113.1	131.1	160.5	2.4	2.6	3.1
MARTINSVILLE CITY AREA	103.8	116.3	102.6	7.5	8.1	8.4
GALAX CITY AREA	91.8	84.0	73.2	0.6	0.7	1.6
PETERSBURG CITY AREA	84.5	67.6	56.3	14.4	15.4	17.1
ROCKBRIDGE COUNTY	82.2	81.4	80.8	2.0	2.2	3.8
SMYTH COUNTY	69.0	67.9	74.8	7.4	8.1	9.7
PRINCE WILLIAM COUNTY	65.3	74.7	76.1	35.4	44.1	64.9
LOUDOUN COUNTY	61.2	62.3	73.4	14.1	17.2	25.5
SALEM CITY AREA	59.7	60.7	73.1	5.5	6.4	7.5
CULPEPER COUNTY	55.6	55.1	55.6	17.8	18.3	22.2
SOUTHBOSTON CITY AREA	52.8	49.7	56.8	2.3	2.4	2.4
HARRISONBURG CITY AREA	51.2	52.6	54.7	35.8	34.7	33.4
BUENAVISTA CITY AREA	50.0	42.9	40.3	0.4	0.5	0.6
FRANKLIN COUNTY	46.9	57.4	65.1	10.9	11.6	12.7
LOUISA COUNTY	45.6	41.4	59.2	7.9	8.8	9.3

RICHMOND COUNTY	40.6	33.5	29.7	8.5	8.2	7.7
WYTHE COUNTY	35.6	37.7	41.9	6.2	6.8	8.7
BEDFORD CITY AREA	34.6	33.9	34.7	2.0	2.3	2.4
PATRICK COUNTY	34.1	33.8	39.8	3.4	3.9	4.3
ACCOMACK COUNTY	33.7	79.2	117.1	2.7	3.4	4.5
FREDERICKSBURG CITY AREA	29.2	35.8	33.8	18.0	18.9	18.7
EMPORIA CITY AREA	26.5	26.9	27.6	1.7	1.8	1.9
CARROLL COUNTY	22.9	23.4	25.8	2.0	2.2	2.7
PRINCE EDWARD COUNTY	20.8	25.0	30.7	6.4	6.5	7.0
STAUNTON CITY AREA	20.4	21.3	24.2	6.1	6.5	7.9
PITTSYLVANIA COUNTY	20.4	34.6	58.3	2.8	3.4	6.3
GRAYSON COUNTY	20.2	18.6	15.3	1.3	1.4	1.9
COLONIALHEIGHTS CITY	18.6	20.3	18.7	5.6	5.8	6.5
SHENANDOAH COUNTY	16.8	41.2	64.9	6.7	7.7	11.3
LEE COUNTY	16.6	16.0	13.6	1.2	1.2	1.7
SPOTSYLVANIA COUNTY	16.1	13.7	11.5	12.4	14.1	20.0
RUSSELL COUNTY	14.4	21.5	21.5	2.3	3.2	4.1
SUSSEX COUNTY	13.6	22.9	22.8	1.2	1.3	1.5
LUNENBURG COUNTY	11.2	10.4	10.1	1.0	1.1	1.2
BRUNSWICK COUNTY	10.5	12.6	14.2	2.2	2.6	3.7
ARLINGTON COUNTY	10.0	79.7	96.1	18.8	23.0	72.7
NOTTOWAY COUNTY	10.0	9.7	9.7	1.4	1.5	1.8
PULASKI COUNTY	9.6	10.0	11.2	3.5	5.7	7.8
FAUQUIER COUNTY	6.7	14.0	13.6	9.6	10.7	12.3
STAFFORD COUNTY	6.7	9.4	8.7	17.3	18.3	22.8
CAROLINE COUNTY	6.4	9.4	8.6	1.3	1.5	3.5
ORANGE COUNTY	5.4	7.6	7.3	1.2	1.2	1.5
NELSON COUNTY	4.1	6.4	5.6	0.4	0.6	0.8
BUCKINGHAM COUNTY	3.7	4.8	4.9	1.3	1.3	1.4
NEWKENT COUNTY	3.5	3.5	3.6	1.0	1.0	1.1
AMHERST COUNTY	2.9	20.3	92.3	0.7	0.7	1.7
FLOYD COUNTY	2.5	5.4	5.8	1.0	1.3	1.5
NORTHAMPTON COUNTY	2.1	2.5	2.2	2.9	3.4	5.7
LANCASTER COUNTY	2.0	2.0	2.0	0.6	0.7	1.1
HIGHLAND COUNTY	1.8	1.6	1.3	0.1	0.1	0.1
KINGAND QUEEN COUNTY	1.6	1.9	2.4	0.3	0.3	0.8
AMELIA COUNTY	1.2	1.4	1.9	3.0	3.3	3.4
LEXINGTON CITY AREA	0.8	1.1	0.9	2.2	2.5	2.7
MIDDLESEX COUNTY	0.7	0.8	0.9	1.3	1.4	1.6
WASHINGTON						
CLARK COUNTY	351.6	372.3	460.6	160.9	168.9	188.6
SPOKANE COUNTY	346.5	464.5	567.9	169.2	184.8	212.7
PIERCE COUNTY	293.1	359.3	608.4	536.2	568.1	623.1
KING COUNTY	220.9	1307.1	2654.3	1129.4	1280.2	1574.1
YAKIMA COUNTY	190.1	194.4	210.4	70.3	79.6	91.3
GRANT COUNTY	139.3	142.8	153.6	43.5	47.5	52.7
GRAYSHARBOR COUNTY	129.8	146.6	158.7	126.0	127.1	124.7
CHELAN COUNTY	97.3	97.4	104.5	14.8	18.1	26.5
THURSTON COUNTY	55.1	85.2	118.0	121.6	131.1	147.3
COWLITZ COUNTY	51.7	156.9	225.1	47.7	49.7	53.1
LEWIS COUNTY	42.1	45.0	47.7	35.2	38.7	47.0
KITTITAS COUNTY	29.0	29.6	29.7	18.0	19.6	23.5
WALLAWALLA COUNTY	26.0	41.4	51.9	46.0	47.0	48.0
KITSAP COUNTY	23.6	26.2	28.1	108.1	115.6	127.6
STEVENS COUNTY	18.7	38.0	53.1	22.8	24.6	27.5
OKANOGAN COUNTY	14.9	19.4	19.2	32.4	32.3	34.3
SKAMANIA COUNTY	8.8	12.0	12.7	4.0	4.2	5.2
PACIFIC COUNTY	3.8	7.5	12.2	9.0	10.1	11.1

WEST VIRGINIA						
CABELL COUNTY	254.3	257.8	255.2	107.7	106.2	103.4
MONONGALIA COUNTY	105.5	110.3	136.0	30.8	30.8	34.7
MASON COUNTY	53.4	77.8	79.0	4.7	5.1	5.8
UPSHUR COUNTY	49.3	47.0	43.2	9.2	10.6	12.0
WAYNE COUNTY	48.8	54.5	79.8	11.1	12.9	14.0
MERCER COUNTY	47.0	45.1	46.4	103.3	101.9	99.7
GRANT COUNTY	34.5	30.2	39.6	18.6	17.8	16.8
HARRISON COUNTY	20.6	22.4	24.8	11.1	12.3	14.7
RALEIGH COUNTY	16.2	15.4	13.6	17.7	20.5	23.4
RANDOLPH COUNTY	14.3	16.4	19.9	3.6	4.1	5.7
PRESTON COUNTY	13.4	13.0	14.9	2.6	3.2	5.5
ROANE COUNTY	4.9	5.5	5.1	46.6	44.6	42.2
MINGO COUNTY	4.5	4.2	4.5	24.1	26.1	26.1
MORGAN COUNTY	2.7	2.3	2.0	4.7	4.8	4.9
BOONE COUNTY	2.4	2.4	2.7	5.2	5.5	6.5
POCAHONTAS COUNTY	1.6	2.0	2.4	1.5	2.6	3.2
WEBSTER COUNTY	1.3	1.5	2.4	2.1	2.4	2.7
BRAXTON COUNTY	0.3	0.4	0.7	3.9	4.0	4.8
WISCONSIN						
MILWAUKEE COUNTY	3893.2	3604.4	3577.8	908.7	996.2	1170.9
WAUKESHA COUNTY	1742.7	1794.2	1913.5	161.7	173.6	199.7
RACINE COUNTY	1348.8	1272.4	1233.0	65.4	73.4	85.5
BROWN COUNTY	940.5	859.9	935.1	171.4	182.9	201.7
ROCK COUNTY	718.2	775.5	837.9	118.3	124.5	126.8
WINNEBAGO COUNTY	605.0	693.4	791.0	60.5	64.0	70.7
OUTAGAMIE COUNTY	598.5	690.7	785.2	121.2	123.8	131.7
SHEBOYGAN COUNTY	499.4	552.5	633.7	70.4	73.0	79.1
JEFFERSON COUNTY	435.9	439.1	459.0	47.2	49.0	53.2
CHIPPEWA COUNTY	412.5	418.8	509.1	39.9	42.3	46.1
DANE COUNTY	403.2	434.3	505.0	214.1	222.9	244.4
DODGE COUNTY	384.0	413.5	459.3	55.1	55.8	57.4
MANITOWOC COUNTY	307.5	306.1	316.6	58.8	61.1	64.7
WASHINGTON COUNTY	295.1	275.5	305.8	125.3	123.3	123.9
PORTAGE COUNTY	254.9	293.7	312.3	36.3	38.0	41.2
MARATHON COUNTY	239.8	290.2	359.4	125.9	132.0	134.9
WALWORTH COUNTY	225.9	238.3	265.5	120.1	119.0	118.3
KENOSHA COUNTY	209.7	255.1	251.0	114.2	113.9	116.3
FONDDULAC COUNTY	185.2	184.6	197.6	80.5	81.2	82.5
OZAUKEE COUNTY	170.6	170.8	186.9	33.1	34.4	39.2
COLUMBIA COUNTY	162.1	157.9	178.8	38.8	38.5	40.4
WOOD COUNTY	154.8	194.8	266.9	64.6	66.7	70.8
MARINETTE COUNTY	144.4	137.5	146.2	31.9	33.2	35.4
MONROE COUNTY	137.8	124.9	128.9	16.2	17.9	20.0
LINCOLN COUNTY	132.4	135.6	166.6	13.0	13.6	13.8
EAUCLAIRE COUNTY	127.4	121.6	112.3	90.5	93.5	93.8
WAUPACA COUNTY	125.5	131.7	161.6	24.1	26.8	31.5
GRANT COUNTY	103.9	111.0	165.1	33.0	34.5	37.5
CALUMET COUNTY	95.9	95.1	102.4	24.6	25.0	25.6
GREEN COUNTY	90.5	139.4	160.2	24.8	26.1	26.9
RICHLAND COUNTY	87.5	75.3	67.8	17.7	17.7	18.0
SAUK COUNTY	87.2	109.7	132.1	37.4	37.8	41.2
ST.CROIX COUNTY	72.9	80.8	100.0	30.9	32.8	37.6
GREENLAKE COUNTY	65.8	57.7	55.3	21.3	22.2	22.7
DOOR COUNTY	65.2	59.9	54.1	31.6	32.0	33.5
OCONTO COUNTY	54.9	56.6	56.7	26.3	27.2	28.6
JUNEAU COUNTY	50.5	50.5	55.4	18.5	18.8	19.1
LANGLADE COUNTY	42.5	36.8	33.9	15.6	15.8	16.2

POLK COUNTY	40.8	40.2	42.7	36.4	37.2	40.0
BARRON COUNTY	39.2	63.8	97.5	32.7	35.7	38.4
SHAWANO COUNTY	35.7	46.7	57.3	24.3	24.6	25.8
BURNETT COUNTY	34.0	34.1	40.1	10.7	10.8	11.2
ASHLAND COUNTY	23.8	25.4	27.6	10.2	11.0	12.4
KEWAUNEE COUNTY	23.7	23.8	24.4	17.8	17.5	17.7
RUSK COUNTY	22.5	19.5	17.7	13.5	13.8	14.3
VERNON COUNTY	16.9	14.7	15.1	22.6	22.7	23.0
PIERCE COUNTY	16.1	14.3	13.7	35.2	36.8	37.9
TREMPEALEAU COUNTY	14.3	26.6	39.8	35.5	36.2	36.5
MARQUETTE COUNTY	12.7	17.9	25.1	7.0	7.2	7.7
CLARK COUNTY	11.5	16.6	19.9	22.5	23.2	25.3
VILAS COUNTY	9.0	9.5	8.4	8.2	8.7	9.9
LAFAYETTE COUNTY	8.4	7.8	7.7	20.3	20.3	20.4
JACKSON COUNTY	7.4	7.7	9.2	10.2	11.4	12.9
FOREST COUNTY	4.2	4.3	4.4	14.4	15.1	16.2
BUFFALO COUNTY	4.0	4.0	4.6	15.5	15.7	16.2
WAUSHARA COUNTY	2.8	3.5	4.5	7.4	7.3	7.5
BAYFIELD COUNTY	2.3	2.4	2.4	9.8	10.5	11.7
PEPIN COUNTY	2.2	1.8	1.5	8.1	8.5	8.9
WYOMING						
SWEETWATER COUNTY	140.3	137.7	166.3	170.7	168.3	161.7
PARK COUNTY	30.4	24.8	20.6	38.2	40.4	41.9
UINTA COUNTY	11.2	11.5	12.4	85.7	86.0	82.6
CROOK COUNTY	3.5	5.0	5.8	9.9	11.2	12.1
WASHAKIE COUNTY	2.3	1.8	1.5	13.2	13.1	12.6

www.ingramcontent.com/pod-product-compliance
Lightning Source LLC
Chambersburg PA
CBHW081602170526
45166CB00009B/2786